W9-AFL-482

Sacraments of Love

A Prayer Journal

ANDREW M. GREELEY

CROSSROAD • NEW YORK

1994

The Crossroad Publishing Company
370 Lexington Avenue, New York, NY 10017

Copyright © 1994 by Andrew M. Greeley

Printed in the United States of America

Library of Congress Cataloging-in-Publication Data

Greeley, Andrew M., 1928–
    Sacraments of love : a prayer journal / Andrew M. Greeley.
      p. cm.
    ISBN 0-8245-1398-3
    1. Greeley, Andrew M., 1928– —Diaries. 2. Catholic Church—
Clergy—Diaries. 3. Spiritual journals. I. Title.
BX4705.G6185A3 1994
248.3'2—dc20   93–40250
                                                      CIP

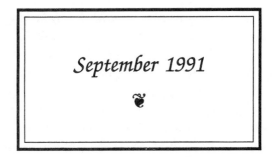

September 1991

September 21, 1991 — Grand Beach, Mich.

My Love,

Yesterday was a day of wonder and surprise for which I am very grateful. First, the Chicago Oceanarium and then the dazzling Circus of the Sun: the splendor of Your creation in the beluga whales and smiling dolphins; the whimsy of Your imagination in the playful circus performers!

I wonder often why there are so many and so complex creatures on just one minor (we presume) planet. And I come up with the same conclusion whenever I consider this splendor: You do it because You *can* do it! You love to show off, to give us a hint of Your own elaborate, complex, and dazzling glory!

"You humans wonder what I'm like," I hear You saying. "Well look at the harbor seal and the sea otter as well as the beluga and the dolphin! Could anyone without a great sense of humor, a love of fun, and a wild imagination have come up with such marvelous creatures?"

You win!

What struck me about the very modern, not to say funky, Circus of the Sun was how much the performers were of the same sort who date back to the Commedia in Italy and Rome and Greece and probably to prehistory — jugglers, tumblers, contortionists, clowns, pantomime artists, acrobats — some of the oldest traditions in the human condition. You made us even more wonderful, and more odd, than the whales and the dolphins!

Each of us, all of us, are sacraments of Your love. Thank You.
I love You.

September 22, 1991 — Grand Beach

My Love,

It's a rainy Sunday morning, the last day of summer and only
a week more up here before I return to Chicago. I thank You for
the gift of this summer house. Now comes the melancholy task of
closing up.

Nothing lasts forever, not even life itself. Only Your love lasts.
I do believe that. Please strengthen my belief.

St. Paul this morning (Philippians) talks about the various
ways of serving You and Your Son, some good, some not so good.
I wish I could be as confident as he is that my service is untainted.
Maybe, to be fair, he isn't all that confident either.

I'm certainly not tied up with the institution against whose
ideologies and oppressions Jean Sulivan continues to rage in his
book *Morning Light* (what am I going to do for spiritual reading
when he is finished?). But there is also the risk of idolatry in being
anti-institutional.

The man quoted in the *New York Times* yesterday who at-
tacked my *America* article on Catholic conservatives was pretty
nasty. He hadn't read the article, but he knew that it was false and
that I write dirty novels, which he hadn't read either, I'm sure.

He writes like a man who is a prisoner of institution worship.
I am not of that sort, surely. And yet I affirm constantly the indis-
pensable nature, indeed the sacramentality, of the institution.

But it's easy for me to be a dissident. The establishment
doesn't pay me. It has nothing I want anymore. I would be terribly unhappy to be caught up in its silly games. Hence my dissent
in the name of honesty and integrity is simple enough.

I must never think that therefore I am virtuous and that those
who do not dissent are cowards. It is not up to me to judge
anyone.

Help me to understand these truths and to try to live by them.
I love You.

September 23, 1991 — Grand Beach

My Love,
Autumn began about two and a half hours ago. I'm in a good mood, eager to return to Chicago and begin my autumn life in that city — with more research on the sociology of prayer. It's always the case, isn't it, that after summer dies I rise quickly to the new and pleasant life of Fall? I hope and I believe that such an experience is a sacrament of the final death that will be followed in some fashion beyond my powers of imagination in the final resurrection.

I want to reflect on what Sulivan says on church institutions today. He's harsh and French but probably right, save in some minor details:

"If the Church were an army, the hierarchical system as it now functions would be extremely efficient. For the strength of an army is generally related to the commitment and ambitions of its officers and junior officers....

"But the Church is nothing like an army. If its leaders are merely a driving belt, powered, whether they know it or not, by fear, making them look first to see how the wind blows or are driven by some vanity that may have the appearance of obedience and devotion, they are only caricatures of the apostles. No communion is built on directives and on compromise but on an inner experience of liberation."

September 25, 1991 — Grand Beach

My Love,
The danger I see for myself in the Sulivan pericope I'm reading today is the risk of self-promotion. I speak out on a lot of subjects, often with lots of backup data. I try to keep my motives reasonably pure: It is good for people to hear a priest who is both loyal and free say what needs to be said; someone has to speak up; my writing has had a positive impact on many people's lives.

All well and good. And I'd like to think I'd keep my mouth shut if the motives weren't valid. But it is very tricky to distinguish between self-promotion and being an outspoken com-

mentator. Moreover, which June Rosner [publicist] seeks a TV
program for me, I have even more reason to be uneasy. TV is
an unbeatable pulpit but also a danger in the world of mass
communication.

I would put aside the risk of self-promotion (and also be free
of criticism) if I did indeed shut up. I would also placate the cardinal and the clerical culture. But that would be infidelity to my
vocation and to the freedom You have bestowed on me; it would
be a simplistic response to a complex issue. So the only proper
behavior, I guess, is to continue to play the game and watch for
the dangers; or perhaps to realize that if one plays the game, one
succumbs at least on occasion to the marginal temptations.

I don't have a Maggie Daley to keep me humble like my
friend [Mayor Richard Daley] down the beach does.

So, if it be Your will and for the good of the good news, then
let the TV project succeed. And, if I should do it, let me do it like
the professional I ought to be in Your service. But if it is not for
Your good, then let it fail.

I love You.

September 26, 1991 — Grand Beach

My Love,

In reading Sulivan and St. Paul this morning — nice contrast,
huh? — it again became clear to me, perhaps clearer than it has
ever been, that the core of my priestly vocation at this time is to
be a storyteller. That ought not to be a great revelation, but somehow it is. I mean, it has hit me as though for the first time that
this is the most important work I do, the one that has the greatest
influence on the largest number of people. Everything else is sec-
ondary. Yet much of the fun has gone out it, not because people
don't like the stories, or because I don't enjoy writing them, but
because of the business surrounding it all.

I paid my dues to storytelling, that's certain. I could stop now
and devote my time to sociology and anything else I want to
do. But I would sooner write stories that reveal Your grace, Your
sacraments of everyday life, than anything else.

If I think of retiring, as I may in the next year and a half as I approach sixty-five, it will not be from storytelling.

Peace and joy, of which St. Paul talks, will not come by not writing any more stories.

Help me to understand this and to take heart about this, my most important and joyous vocation.

September 27, 1991 — Grand Beach

My Love,

Some poems began to flow yesterday afternoon. It's a strange experience to hear the words in my head and then put them down on this screen, even stranger than to hear and see the progress of a story. Moreover, once I am able to release my ego, the metaphors flow too. An astonishing process!

The poems are prayers. Better yet, they are *angst*-dismissing prayers. They help me to resolve some of the problems that are troubling me. I should do them more often because they are a grace. Writing them is a thrilling, grace-full experience.

Thank You!

I love You very much!

September 28, 1991 — Grand Beach

My Love,

Last night President Bush ordered the end of all American short-range missiles — a political move doubtless, but also a sign of the times. The cold war is over, the nuclear risk is diminished. All the prophets of doom were wrong. Peace is assured at least for the time. What a marvel! Have we given You enough thanks for this transformation, for this dramatic end not only of the cold war but of World War II?

I love You. Thank You.

September 29, 1991 — Grand Beach

My Love,

This is the last of my reflections at Grand Beach this year, save for an occasional weekend later on. After I've finished, I'll pull the computer out of the docking station and pack it for return to Chicago.

I am grateful for all the blessings of this summer — the weather, the friends, the waterskiing, the Masses on weekends, the walks on the beach, the swimming — all the good things which I don't deserve but which help me to stay vigorous and healthy.

Also I'm grateful for all the work I've done during this last month here. I'm eager to get back to Chicago just as I regret the passing of the summer. But life moves on. For all of life I am grateful.

Help me to relax during the rush and excitement of the next three months in town, the six flights around the country and the world.

I love You.

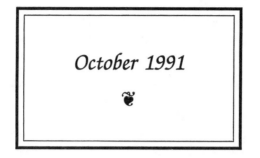

October 1991

October 1, 1991 — Chicago

My Love,

Back in Chicago as autumn begins and as tight as a drum as I try to adjust. It isn't easy. The work piles up. I read this morning some poetry by a former priest. He seems to regret what is something less than perfect marriage, and he laments for the priesthood lost. I suspect that like a lot of priests he expected more from marriage than it has to give. Only four years into it and already disillusioned. More honest about it than most. I have empathy for the man and a renewed sense of the value of the priesthood for me. I wonder if some of the younger priests value it for what it's worth or whether that value has been lost and must be recaptured again.

Thank You for the strength of commitment. Help me to always value the gift and the grace which supports it.

I love You.

October 4, 1991 — Wilkes Barre, Pa.

My Love,

It's a lovely day on the banks of the Susquehanna river, and the countryside is beautiful as the leaves turn red and gold. I'm off to Elizabethtown College tonight to complete this mini-lecture tour. I've been sitting in the hotel room all day working on my article about the Irish for the social science encyclopedia. It's the disciplined use of time which enables me to get things done even when I travel — charts, columns, and articles.

It also means that I'm kind of tired. But I'd be tired even if I didn't sit here and work and instead went out and toured the countryside and learned more about this old and interesting region of our country — one in which the Catholic Church often seems to the right of Innocent III. My talk was very well received last night, and I'm grateful. Somehow I've become the "voice of reason and compassion in the church," a change from ten for fifteen years ago when many people wrote me off as a reactionary. I haven't changed but I guess the church has. Well, maybe I have changed. If so, it's the stories that did it.

Anyway, I am grateful for the warmth of the experience and for the sense that I really do represent the Catholic tradition at its best on nights like this. Help me to do as well down in Elizabethtown tonight and bring me home to Chicago tomorrow morning safe and well.

I love You.

October 6, 1991 — Chicago

I slept on the plane, I slept after I arrived at the apartment, and I slept soundly last night. I wonder again why I bother with such lectures. The talk itself is almost always fun, the audience reaction positive, and I feel good about what I've done and confident of my work. Yet I'm exhausted when it's over and I don't think I've accomplished very much except to give some encouragement to discouraged Catholics and some illumination to non-Catholics. I mustn't write those achievements off and I'm grateful for them, but what impact do they have on eternity?

I guess the answer is, what impact does anything have?

Anyway, I continue to give them, more of them for free than not for free. And I'll continue to give them while You give me life and health. And I'll leave the impact to Your grace, which is all I can do anyway.

Someone said in the last few days that all of life is a preparation for aging. In a certain sense that is true, though in a wider sense it is an old person's comment and ignores much else in life. I reject it in the most pessimistic sense, but beginning tomorrow I will reflect on it in the restricted and, I think, more optimistic sense.

Now off to the Bears game, which will be an exercise in frustration and futility!

October 8, 1991 — Chicago

My Love,

A bad day coming up: an early breakfast meeting, then the dentist, and after that a luncheon. And I think I'm getting a migraine headache!

Anyway, about old age: You know the saying that there is no one more dead than a dead priest. It is also true, I think, that there is no one more lonely than an old priest. I watched an elderly man in the pool yesterday, a stroke victim it would seem. His wife patiently helped him in and out of the pool — though in it he navigated pretty well.

If that happens to me, there will be no one to help.

I take reasonably good care of my health, don't drink much or smoke at all, win the weight battle (not easy), exercise, and do all the good things one is supposed to do. Dr. Phee tells me I have lucked out on the genes. Yet eventually aging will catch up with me. I will be forced to be patient with my physical and emotional ills, to accept the deterioration of my faculties, to live with a drift back towards childhood.

So be it. I ask You to spare me whatever can be spared, but I accept whatever will happen.

I should practice now being patient, especially with things like elevators in this building and traffic lights and other things which upset me — senselessly and needlessly.

Patience is the word, and I need a lot of it now. I'll probably need even more in the years to come.

I love You, no matter what happens.

October 9, 1991 — Chicago

My Love,

Yesterday, with three hours in the dentist chair, was even worse than I had expected it to be. I'm still a basket case this morning as I get ready for another rough day. Well, teeth trouble is part of growing old, except I've had it all my life. It's one of the bad things about being Irish, but there are so many good things about it that I'll put up with the bad without too much complaint.

I received from Brother Dietrich yesterday a copy of Kathleen Hughes life of Godfrey Diekmann. It looks like a wonderful book. The final quote from Godfrey compares You to music. *God is music.* How wonderful! And how true!

You are rhythm and melody and harmony and sweetness and light and brass and horn and viola all combined in wonderful symphony. Music maybe more than anything else. Music who is a person, music who is a lover, music who is a gift of Self!

I do believe that, even in my present attenuated condition. Help me to believe it more and more and continue my efforts today to be patient.

October 10, 1991 — Chicago

My Love,

The present moment is sacred ground, Whitehead observed. And the spiritual author I'm reading today raises the question of whether the present person is also sacred ground.

That's a very powerful thought — the sacredness, the holiness of the present. Today, with a student appointment, lunch with David Tracy, an autographing with Jack Egan, phone calls, mail, a ride to the university, etc., etc., is a sacred day. There are opportunities for encountering grace and being graceful that will never happen again. To take advantage of these opportunities will require an awareness of Your presence and an awareness that I am You when dealing with others, that I must show them the love You show me, for they are You also.

Help me always to be generous and loving and good to all I encounter. I love You.

October 11, 1991 — Chicago

My Love,
The pedophile story finally broke last night on channel 5. The archdiocese had tried a slick, spin-control trick and Mary Anne Ahern finally had it with their dishonesty. I'm sure there'll be tremendous pressure on the news media to back off. I hope they stick to their guns.

This stuff has to stop, the victimization, the persecution of the victims and their families, the cover-ups, the terrible stigma on the priesthood — it all has to stop! Please grant the cardinal the wisdom and the courage to do it right this time.

I'll probably send him a letter over the weekend, begging him to do it right.

I was instrumental in setting Mary Anne loose yesterday, though indirectly so she wouldn't know for sure it was me. She's smart enough to have guessed. I'm happy that I did so, because not to be concerned about the terrible things the church is doing to its people would be sinful, especially when I am free to speak out. I must resist the temptation to be too self-satisfied about it all. I'm so glad it's out in the open at last and I'm not the only one who is carrying the ball.

I want to pray this morning for the victims and the victimizers, who themselves were also victims. Please help them and please help the church.

October 13, 1991 — Chicago

My Love,
St. Paul warns that we do not know the time of the Lord's coming and the Irish poems I also read this morning — the buried at Clonmacnoise, Paddy Kavanagh's epitaph — also remind me that my death cannot be so far away.

Somber thought, but true, so true.

I was insulted three times at the Irish heritage center yesterday, each time by a real Irishman as opposed to an Irish American. The classic put-down of a culture still haunted by self-hatred.

Yet what will these mean when I'm dead. What will the false stories about my novels mean? What will all the work I've done mean? In a few years my work and I will be forgotten just as are the men buried beneath the meadows at Clonmacnoise.

Intellectually I know that to be true and I accept it. Yet I charge through life as though what I did mattered enormously. My work matters, indeed, but not all that much, not enough to worry about or become frantic over. I must prepare for death. And I must do so by valuing life and also by being prepared to lose it so that I may be born again.

I do believe that. Help such belief to permeate my life.

I love You.

October 15, 1991 — Chicago

My Love,

I've been reading 1 Thessalonians the last couple of mornings, the first recorded words of Christianity, written less than two decades after Your Son returned to You. I'm struck by a couple of things. First of all, it is a much simpler St. Paul than one encounters in later years and one who seems to expect the return of Your Son sooner rather than later. Moreover, despite the short time since his departure, there is already a strongly developed Christology, which seems to me to get in the way of the good news. Already the messenger seems more important than the message. I'm not complaining about St. Paul. He said what he thought best to say in his time and place, but the message of Your love seems to be somehow lost in the message about the Lordship of Jesus. One can hardly imagine that Jesus, who so fiercely insisted on the message, would be pleased.

But we've been doing that every since, have we not? We have been so concerned about questions of power and institution and orthodoxy and sexuality that we have lost sight of the central message of love. One sees little compassion in the behavior of either the Chicago chancery or the Vatican. Means have become ends and ends have been forgotten. Not that I'm all that good at it myself. How much of my work as a priest, which is intended to preach the good news, has been hung up on less ultimate goals.

Help me to keep my priorities straight in these busy days.
I love You.

October 16, 1991 — Chicago

My Love,
The Irish poem I read today (translated from the medieval) pleads that I may never be separated from Your sweetness. Good thought. The poet sees the sweetness of God particularly in the sweetness of nature, but I would add Your sweetness is everywhere, in nature, in cities, in human friendships and love, in works of art like the Mozart opera (*Figaro*) that I'm going to see tonight. Those who deny Your existence because of the problem of evil are at a loss to contend with the far more serious problem of good. Why is there good and truth and beauty in the world or indeed anywhere?

I believe that it all reflects Someone. If it doesn't, then why is there anything at all? How come?

That is the question finally, isn't it? How come? How come me, how come others, how come world? All an accident or a chance or a deceit? That doesn't seem very likely, does it?

So, if there be so much sweetness, there must be Sweetness. From that sweetness never let me be separated.

And thanks for the opportunity to hear Mozart — one of the great gifts of Your sweetness.

October 17, 1991 — Chicago

My Love,
Mozart was wonderful yesterday, just marvelous — human comedy, dazzling music, and deep moral sensitivity. What a genius he was! I'm treating myself to a day off today and riding out to the arboretum for a visit to the forest and the prairies, a last touch of Indian summer. I am grateful for the arboretum and Indian summer and the time to ride out there.

The Irish poems today, particularly Seamus Heaney's, are about generations, about his debt to his father and his grandfather. I didn't know any of my grandparents and my father has been gone for forty-four years this autumn. I hardly remember him. I admired him greatly and was not close to him, mostly because he was so tied up in financial problems caused by the Great Depression and then exhausted by his long ride to work when I was a teen. Obviously he made a great impression on me because I am so much like him in so many ways, including the determined integrity I never thought I had but which still drives me to the fringes of the institutional church.

So I guess, like Seamus, I am digging in the same fields in which he dug. I don't regret that. Will any of what I have done, that on which I have worked so hard, last?

I can't sort any of it out, to tell the truth. The only explanation I can put on things is that I trust You to make up for my weaknesses, so long as I try hard to do my best.

And for that I love You even more.

October 18, 1991 — Chicago

My Love,

I have not had a chance since my talk at Northwestern on Tuesday to reflect on [Fr.] John Krump's death. John was, when it was all said and done, my closest friend in the class who remained a priest and perhaps in a way my only friend, the only one who understood what I was doing and admired it. I miss him and Dan Herr terribly. Grant them peace and happiness and grant that we might all some day be together again.

I reflect this morning, as I continue to rush about, on the fact that I have written on prayer and do not pray enough. Indeed these reflections are prayers but my morning and night prayers and my prayers as I leave and come back to the apartment are slipping. I must try to return to them if I take my own sociology of prayer seriously. How can the only sociologist of prayer in the world not pray more often?

Please help me to do better. And please help me to enjoy the Emerald Ball tonight.

I love You.

October 21, 1991 — Chicago

My Love,

"Brightness of brightness" is what the Irish poet calls the woman he met on the hillside. I'm not sure whether the woman is a real woman or, more likely, Ireland, Kathleen Ni Houlihan herself! But he has so idealized her that whether she is Kathy or Kathleen, she's more than human, a sacrament of You.

Great image and one which, surprisingly, has escaped Christianity. Mary is, of course, the sacrament par excellence of Your love, the Mother love of God, but her image as Spouse has been so desexualized that the human experience of erotic beauty has been robbed of its sacramental dimension. Admittedly the desired spouse is also a sacrament, but not one that is *really* and physically desired. We have yet to integrate sexual appeal into our sacramentality, for obvious reasons of prudishness and fear of women, but it's high time that we did.

A beautiful person of either sex is a sacrament of You who are all-beautiful and all-appealing. Both feminist ideology and puritanism fight that truth, so it doesn't stand much chance in the church just yet, but at least I can understand that beauty (which endures despite age) gives me a hint of You, a God who entices and calls, a God who wants to win us with attractiveness.

What a liberating idea that would be for men and women, especially young men and women.

Can I preach on this? I'll try.

Most of my work for the year is done. I'm caught up. Now what will I do with my time? It will be interesting to see. First of all, I'm going to read.

I love You.

October 23, 1991 — Chicago

My Love,

The Irish poem I read this morning makes me think of the simple life, a thought particularly appealing after the barrage of phone calls both here and at the office all day yesterday. A simple life I do not live, neither in my work or activities nor in my living arrangements — four careers, three homes, many projects, several crusades.

This Indian summer morning with the temperature going into the eighties I wonder whether I would do it all again, would I try so many different things, would I extend myself in so many commitments and acquire so many resources. Was, for example, the color printer, so effective for presentations but so much effort to master, worth the time and energy? Could not that question be asked of all the paraphernalia of things which I have acquired and which I will not be able to take with me when I die? And the work on prayer in the *Sun Times* — an interesting project but working on the rewrite yesterday ate up much of the day. The sociology of prayer is an interesting field, but did I need to get into it?

And the terrible pedophile cases, which occupy an increasing amount of my time, is that my battle?

Why can't I say no to more things and ideas?

Is it necessary for me to read five newspapers every day?

So it goes: all good questions and no good answers. I've got to think about these things in days to come and ask myself why I should be doing so much and whether it would not be better for me to cut back and to simplify my life.

Why should I try to see so many people on my trip to Washington and New York for example — four different people or couples during a day and a half in Washington? Or why the trip to Boston?

What sense does it all make?

Tomorrow, my Love, I will try to answer all these questions or begin to answer them.

October 28, 1991 — Chicago

My Love,

I have been away from these reflections for a few days, as You well know, because I didn't bring my computer with me on the trip to Ann Arbor.

Once more the public address system didn't work, the third

time in a row. I can't understand why people go to all the trouble of having a speaker and then don't check their PA.

So I am feeling used again, treated like a commodity that attracts people and not like a person. Except for the trip to Ireland, which is for a book that I want to write, my trips this autumn are to do favors for others. I sometimes feel exploited. Of course the reason — perhaps the main reason — is that I don't treat myself with adequate respect. I exploit my own talents — write a quick blessing or a quick review or a quick article or a quick data analysis or even a quick novel in response to demands from someone else. I can't say no.

I treat myself like a machine to produce work to please others. I don't value either the work or the worker nearly enough. I have set up a distance between myself and what I do, which perhaps makes it easier for me to work but which in truth shows little respect for *me*.

I think this is the proper answer to the questions I asked in my last reflection: I don't have enough respect for myself to be able to say no either when others make demands or when I impose them on myself. I am deficient in proper self-love. I sometimes think I've turned myself into a hack.

I don't know what to do about it, but I'll have to pray and ponder over this in the days ahead.

October 29, 1991 — Chicago

My Love,

Still more rain. It's beginning to get to me as it always does. And off to the dentist again today.

Bad night at the party last night. I got into a big argument about the pedophile thing with a priest who lamented the fact that the archdiocese was going to lose lots of money that it didn't have and that the right wing would go after the cardinal because of these matters. Not a hint of concern for the victims. I lost my temper and stormed out.

On this one I may finally break with the priests of the archdiocese who are so much like the one I argued with. They are guilty of being silent accessories and I intend to say so.

Now about me and my lack of respect for myself: I've been so busy these last few days that I haven't had time to think about that subject. I'm trying to slow down the engines, but so far without much success. Please help me to do this a bit more effectively.

I love You. Thank You for loving me.

October 30, 1991 — Chicago

My Love,

I'm kind of hibernating in my apartment on a rainy day with no reason to go out, catching up on my reading and getting over the effects of the dentist yesterday.

There was a call to my office from Ken Villot, the cardinal's secretary, perhaps in response to the letters I've written to him in the last couple of days, pleading with him to do something about the pedophile situation before it's too late.

But I'm skeptical and suspicious. I told Mary [secretary] that if he should call back she should ask what he wanted. I'm happy to talk to Ken as a friend, but not as a cardinal's secretary. If, I told her, the cardinal wants to talk to me, let him call and then give him the phone number here at the apartment.

In the words of Richard J. Daley, let him make the first move. June Rosner thinks I'm being unprofessional. But I know both the way the church works and my own tendency to take church authority more seriously than I should or want to when they get off the phone. Let Joe [Cardinal Bernardin] call me if he wants to talk to me and let him come visit my apartment if he wants to see me. I will not go into that building or up to his house. This is a delicate matter and a delicate time. I want to protect the church from worse harm and I suppose I would not mind some kind of reconciliation with my bishop. But there are dangers in the reconciliation too, dangers that come from the risk of being swept up by ecclesiastical authorities.

I must proceed cautiously, bravely, intelligently, and firmly. Help me to be as wise as a serpent and as prudent as a dove!

I love You.

October 31, 1991 — Chicago

My Love,
   No call from the cardinal's office. False alarm?
   Halloween, a neat holiday. I'll have candy for the kids this evening.
   Faith, Frederick Buechner says in this morning's reading, is the assurance that our very dreams are true after all. How wonderful!
   Yes, they are true! At some level they simply have to be true, don't they?
   We have that instinct, that conviction, probably programmed into us.
   Wish fulfillment? Sure but not necessarily false by that reason. To reflect at all is to encounter beauty and goodness even if we want to deny their existence. To experience at all is to experience hope and dream and wonder and therefore You.
   Even on gray Halloween days!
   Buechner's memoir is so much better than mine, even if mine was a success. He reflects on life rather than trying to describe it. If I do "Confessions of a Parish Priest II," I must do a lot more reflection on the meaning of it. It would be terrible not to. Maybe I had to write the first one to get ready to write the second one!
   Maybe indeed I'll find a lot more value for myself if I do that. Maybe that's the goal.
   I love You.

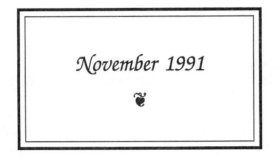

November 1991

November 1, 1991 — Chicago

My Love,

A cold, blustery All Saints' Day. I must talk at the First Friday club today. I hope they give me time to say something more than "hello" and "goodbye" like the last time.

I finished reading *Nora* last night, the biography of James Joyce's wife. It's an astonishing love story. Odd that Joyce, who was bitterly anti-Catholic, was in fact so Catholic in his belief that life was stronger than death and that love was the sign of the strength of life. The book was a profoundly moving story of the human spirit. What a pity the Ireland of his time was incapable of grasping how Catholic he was. There are, of course, lots of explanations, most of them to be traced to the centuries of foreign oppression.

Well, at least we know now what Joyce stood for and that he was right and we can celebrate his Catholicism.

I had a letter yesterday from a man I take to be elderly, though perhaps not too much older than I, about *The Cardinal Virtues*. He enjoyed the book but objected to the "foul" language and equated it with approval of premarital sex. This hang-up on language utterly astonishes me. I really don't know what to make of it. People who are apparently not troubled by the pedophilia in the clergy are shocked by "bad" language.

I wonder who they are trying to kid. Hypocrites and pharisees, I feel like saying to them.

The phone from the chancery was merely about a lost letter. So there! October is over, my work for the year pretty well cleaned up. I'm in the midst of reading and preparing for the trip to Ireland and some Christmas shopping before I go. Help me to keep You in mind — and the image of the Liffey flowing into the ocean only to be reborn again as "riverrun."

November 2, 1991 — Chicago

My Love,

Speaking of being reborn as "riverrun…"

I stormed up to the cardinal's this morning to protest the subpoena, and I left with our friendship renewed!

"I've always wanted to be friends," he said. "I don't know how it happened that we are no longer friends."

I replied that I knew why, that some people resented the friendship and wanted to end it and we let them do so.

He said he was angry and hurt and didn't trust me. I said the same thing. We went over some of the events of the past and laid them to rest. Not all of them perhaps, but enough to begin again. He gave me his number. We will talk privately, not publicly. Maybe the world will be a better place. We need a longer talk, I think, over a dinner to clear the air a bit more. And he has to get rid of that subpoena. But the friendship is renewed. I hope so anyway.

As I walked up there I thought this was a possible outcome. I now wonder why I didn't walk up there long ago. For that I'm sorry. What does it mean for the future?

One step at a time. Please help me take those steps.

And thank You.

November 3, 1991 — Chicago

My Love,

I'm just back from the Bears game at Soldier Field with the Ace in zero windchill weather. Brrr! But we won!

I'm still absorbing the events of yesterday, which still astonish me and — excuse me but a string of birds just passed across the cloudy sky heading south, probably in a rush because they were as surprised by the cold as we are. Dazzling beauty!

I didn't sleep well last night, trying to straighten out my thoughts on reconciliation with Joe. It's a good idea, it's overdue. I had made a lot of mistakes, most of which were the result of storming off in anger. I must be wise about this friendship from now on, not pushing too hard but not being silent either. I'll have to play it by ear, confidently and carefully, not being coopted, but not being too eager to make my opinion known.

Anyway, thank You for the opportunity, the challenge, and the renewal in this new situation. Help me to make the most of it.

Only two more weeks and I'm off to Ireland, less than that actually. Grant that the trip goes well.

I love You.

November 6, 1991 — Chicago

My Love,

I'm on the Midway plane at the airport. This is the third of my six trips during the fall quarter. I've already read all the papers and did my half-hour swim — mostly because I woke up at 4:00 instead of 4:30. With the schedule I have the next three days, I'll probably be a basket case by the time I get home. Anyway, take care of me on this trip and protect me from too much worry about this subpoena business. I don't need it; neither does the cardinal. But I wonder if he can control the men around him, especially the lawyers. Concern for the victims and their families must come first. And only then will the church be able to survive this mess it created itself.

The Buechner book continues to be compelling and troubling — his father's suicide, his discharge from the army, but especially the evocation of that era with all its poignant memories for me. My life was much less traumatic than his. You protected me from many potential troubles by overwhelming me with the desire for the priesthood early in the game. For which many, many thanks.

I'm so conscious these days of the formative power of those years in my life. On the whole it was a benign influence, anchoring me to You very early on, though I haven't lived up to the promise and invitation to love You offered me then and now. In the years remaining, help me to do so. Help me especially during this rush.

I love You.

November 7, 1991 — Washington, D.C.

I'm at National Airport waiting for the shuttle to New York for another talk. It would be so nice if there were an hour or two for sleeping when I get to the hotel in New York. It will be eleven o'clock at the earliest before I get to bed. Anyway, the talk this morning went well, and the cardinal called my office to report (hopefully) that the subpoena would be quashed. Help me to continue what I'd begun and not to become too tired.

November 9, 1991 — Chicago

My Love,

Back in Chicago and recovering from the trip. It was something of a triumphal procession and for that I'm grateful, while at the same time hoping that I understand the risks of self-promotion involved. Help me to steer the proper path through this new minefield and be true to You and to myself.

No phone calls from the cardinal yet. I hope there's not another public fight, but if there is, there is.

The Buechner memoir is disturbing and haunting, mostly because it brings back the era when the two of us were growing up, my life much smoother than his and perhaps much more shallow. I may study prayer and mysticism, but I am not much good at prayer, I fear, and not at all a mystic. The world is too much with me, much too much.

On a Saturday morning like this, tired and eager to loaf, I still have work to do — work, work, work. Why I ask myself — why, why, why? What good does it all do? What does it matter from the point of view of eternity? What does anything I have done or will do matter from the point of view of eternity?

Maybe I should to go bed and sleep and I'll feel better. Maybe I will. But then I wait for the cardinal's call, don't I?

I'm sorry.

November 11, 1991 — Chicago

My Love,

I had a terrible dream on Saturday night, a furiously angry outburst at someone who is not a proper target but whose image drifted across my mind during the day and became an inkblot at night. It was, as You know, a highly creative dream. It revealed the latent anger which still bothers me since the late 1970s and the early 1980s, when my papers were stolen and my name smeared with awful lies and my first friendship with Joe almost destroyed because of it, and which has been summoned up from the depths of my soul because of Joe's offer of reconciliation.

What can I say?

First of all, I have reasons to be angry. Secondly, my anger was and is excessive. And thirdly, it got in the way in the past and it must not get in the way again.

It interfered with my judgment and it will continue to interfere with my judgment if I am not careful. As You know, it remained with me for much of the weekend after the dream and almost caused me to make a serious mistake. I must be wary of it. Forgiving is one thing, and I do that almost too easily, but exorcising anger is something else again and not easy for me to do. At all, at all. Especially when I'm tired or harassed.

Help me through this crisis, I beg You.

November 12, 1991 — Chicago

My Love,

I saw the film *The Rapture* yesterday and I think You have grounds to sue! I can't figure out whether the filmmaker is angry at fundamentalism, at all religion, or at You. However, the portrait of You in the film — a cruel, vindictive, arbitrary God who takes pleasure in playing games with people and then in punishing them — is not altogether foreign to the Catholic tradition either, though it is a depiction of You that fortunately is not fashionable just now.

There is no sign in the film of You as Lover. You are depicted as demanding love, but not loving. Indeed, the theme of the film is that You love us *because* we love You. Our love, in other words, merits Your love.

But that is not the case. *You love because You love us.* We don't earn it, we don't merit it, we don't obtain it in some kind of deal with You. You would not have left that poor troubled woman in the movie forever on the fringes of heaven, especially because it was religion, however limited a religion, that caused her troubles. You would have found a place for her in Your home regardless of what Roger Ebert calls her spiritual pride.

The image of You in that film is as much part of our culture as is the lovely image in *Always* — perhaps more powerful even than the latter image. We have tried to scare too many people for too long into virtue. But You are in fact a God of Love and that seems to have been forgotten all too frequently.

Help me to teach only Your love. "Always."

November 13, 1991 — Chicago

My Love,

I had a very stimulating dinner experience last night at the Jesuit provincial headquarters — a zealous and young provincial and good priests. There is still enormous vitality in the church — faith, creativity, energy, hope. We talked about the priests and nuns who came from Christ the King parish [Fr. Greeley's first assignment] who have done so much good and about my books which have had an impact on those men that I would not have expected. I was dizzy with excitement and gratitude when I left, the excitement over the strength of faith and gratitude to You for what I have been able to accomplish. These are very heady days in a very heady year. I must be careful not to blow it, not by pride, not by copping out, and especially not by needless anger — for any reason.

I'll need a lot of help. I also need to realize that many men and women will be counting on me. I must not let them down.

Please, please help.

And also help me to pray more and more devoutly.

I love You.

November 14, 1991 — Chicago

My Love,

I'll see the cardinal tonight at 8:30, a crucial step in both our renewed friendship and my attempts to head off the pedophile crisis. I must be adroit, prudent, and also very honest. So much is at stake. I will not blow this one by losing my temper again. That act is over. Nor will I be coopted. This may be one of the most important evenings of my life. Help me to do it well.

And help me not to take myself too seriously.

I love You.

November 15, 1991 — Chicago

My Love,

The conversation with the cardinal went well last night, very well indeed, for which many thanks. He's accepting most of my suggestions for dealing with the pedophile crisis. I hope that he gets his report out and everything done properly before more news breaks. He's way ahead of the game compared to other bishops at a comparable stage in the process.

Moreover, we have straightened out our relationship. There is nothing, I told him, that need ever arise between us that cannot be discussed and solved.

He said that he had opposed a book about him that slandered me. He told me how he had frustrated a Vatican attempt to get a condemnation of me and overruled a suggestion from the commission of perhaps writing a column in which he took me mildly to task for the novels. He even told me of [Cardinal] John

O'Connor's support, which gives me pause in my criticism of the Rear Admiral! And he accepted my offer to draft a statement for him on the parish.

We met in a study on the second floor of the house, obviously his, tastefully decorated but with little sign of human inhabitants. He wore a sweater over his collarless shirt, the only kind he seems to have. He introduced me to his sister, who was in town to visit his mother, a very pretty woman maybe in her middle fifties, and told me stories about his mother. He was gentle and soft-spoken as he tends to be in such circumstances. I was impressed by his determination on the pedophile crisis.

I can't claim I've won in that problem. But I've done my part and maybe the victims and their families and the church will win.

Time will tell.

And I'll have to continue to be careful, to watch my new role carefully, not to overplay or underplay.

A nice present as I go off to Ireland. For which many, many thanks.

I love You.

November 16, 1991 — Manchester, England

My Love,

I'm waiting for the Aer Lingus flight to Dublin. It's cold but not raining. I hope You provide good weather for me in Ireland like You usually do. Especially today when the sunlight would be most helpful in fooling my body into adapting to Irish time.

I'm looking forward to this trip for reasons that are not altogether clear to me. Perhaps Dublin has become another home like Tucson and Grand Beach, not a strange place any more.

More reflections on the conversation with Joe. I should have seen him long ago. My anger and resentment and sense of betrayal lasted too long and was misdirected. I need not take all the blame myself, but just the same I wasted many precious years when I could have made a contribution to Chicago and the church. I regret that and I will for the rest of my life. I hope You will forgive me.

There are excuses and I know them all, and all too well. The feelings of assault I experienced in those days and the days after was fearsome. It took me a long time to understand them. I never did comprehend them until just a week or two ago. Maybe I've learned something. I hope so.

I don't dispute Your plans in all of this. I know that You bring good out of everything. I dispute rather my own unduly prolonged anger, and the blindness that came with it.

I thank You for everything.

November 17, 1991 — Dublin, Ireland

My Love,

Well, I must thank You for the sunshine yesterday, which helped notably in the game of tricking by body through my eyes to think that it is living on Dublin time. I feel fine thanks to that sacrament of love.

Dublin continues to fascinate, a "lughly" city as Bold Jimmy Joyce called it. Shrewsbury Road exceeded my expectations. I'll go out wandering again about noontime — with my mandatory stop at Bewleys.

I am very grateful to You for giving me the opportunity to travel, particularly to this addictive city. Help me to keep You in mind and You as the purpose of it all as I wander the city — and to remember all the suffering that others endured that we might be free Irish Catholic Americans. I love You.

November 18, 1991 — Dublin

My Love,

Thank You for the opportunity to visit churches today.

November 19, 1991 — Dublin

My Love,

I was dragged out of my room last night just as I was about to go to bed by the bishop of Ferns [Wexford] who was eating with two other priests in the restaurant here. It was a pleasant conversation.

He didn't tell me this, but I know that he is a good man who was passed over a number of times to be archbishop here in a typically stupid Roman move. Anyway he did want to tell me how much my work had meant to his life. Which was very nice even at eleven o'clock at night — the Irish not being given much to going to bed at reasonable hours.

One more proof this impossible year, if I still needed it, of how much impact my work has had, even in a country where much of it is not known. I have let the reaction in Chicago and especially among priests there blind me to the importance of what I have done. I'm sorry.

In truth, I don't know what to do with this sudden discovery that I'm not the failure I thought I was. I'm glad to know it, of course. I regret my own discouragement and pessimism. And I'm uncertain about how to cope with the information about success — even being a hero away from my own country and my own people. I must not swing from discouragement to arrogance. I guess there's not too much danger of that happening, though the context of my life has suddenly changed and I'm still bemused by it.

Grateful, but bemused.

And I regret, my Love, for so misreading Your plans for me and not showing the affection and gratitude for Your loving vulnerability that I should have shown. I know You forgive me, and I also know that You like to hear me say that I'm sorry.

I DO love You.

November 20, 1991 — Dublin

My Love,

Somehow I missed yesterday. And I've missed today too. I'm sorry. I love You.

Tomorrow I promise I'll sit down first thing.

November 21, 1991 — Dublin

My Love,

Sorry, I'm hurrying again. There's the phone and I must go downstairs to see these folks. I love You. I'll try to get back before the day is over.

Thanks, by the way, for a nice if hurried trip.

November 22, 1991 — Dublin

My Love,

Friday already, the trip is almost over. The fictional part of it is finished, for which much thanks, and the sociological part is less successful because of confusions, but successful enough.

Oddly enough this is the first trip abroad in my life in which I am in no hurry to get home. I hope everything has gone well in Chicago in my absence. Apparently twenty priests have been removed because of pedophilia charges, a high number it seems to me. At least the archdiocese has done something. Now the issue is whether the State's Attorney will do the same thing. I do not think my fellow priests will ever forgive me for advancing this issue. So be it.

All is in Your hands, including the number of years I have left and the survival of my health. I'm grateful for what I've had so far and I love You.

November 24, 1991 — Dublin

My Love,

Last day here. Sorry it's over, but eager to get back home. My fascination with this city and this country grows. Somehow in my plans for a serious novel I must work Ireland into it.

There is a good deal more tragedy in life here than in America. What do I mean by that? I mean poverty surely, but poverty doesn't mean tragedy. The tragedy, I guess, is the result of unrewarded talent and work and the fact that so many people have to leave the country to find the kind of life to which their work and talent entitle them or would entitle them elsewhere.

Then there's the tragedy of the eighteen-year-old woman blown up as she was carrying a Provo bomb in St. Albans in England.

A sad history here, its hand still heavily on the people. I'm lucky that my American version of the heritage has left all that behind.

I wish to pray for the Harmons, with whom I ate last night, and Mary Wheland, at whose home I ate dinner the night before, and of course for the grandnephew, Neil Thomas Montague. Protect them all.

November 26, 1991 — Chicago

It's great to be home. Thank You for bringing me home safely. I am still on overload and must pour on the images in poetry as soon as I can. Maybe on airplanes in the next two weeks. I feel the images of Ireland banging up against the walls of my skull.

The cardinal saw Jeanne Miller last night. I hope against hope that it worked out and that the corner finally has been turned on this pedophile mess. Grant that it works out. I'm also sending him a draft for the statement on the parish. I hope he likes that too.

I read Seamus Heaney on the plane coming home yesterday. His new book of poems is called *Seeing Things*. It's a pun about the various things we see, about *truly* seeing them, seeing what lurks behind them. It is just magnificent verse, well deserving of the Nobel Prize. It is also profoundly Catholic, sometimes explicitly, because of the grace that lurks in the things we see; in fact the book is about the sacramentality of things.

I don't see them much, do I? Not the way Your man Seamus does! There are so many things to see in this city to which I joyously returned. I note them in passing, but have no real sight, or insight into them. Help me to see more clearly, especially as my Advent spiritual exercise.

I love You. Again I'm grateful for the love with which You brought me to Ireland and then home again.

November 27, 1991 — Chicago

My Love,

The conversation between the cardinal and Jeanne Miller went well, for which many thank. And he liked my paper on the parish, for which also many thanks. Now if we can only resolve the Northbrook suit, the core of the pedophile mess will be behind us, and he will have reasserted his leadership role both in the archdiocese and the nation.

And he and I are friends, perhaps cautiously but I think definitively.

Your crooked lines are working very well.

A strange six months, new relationships with the university and the archdiocese. I regret so much time has been wasted in the latter area, but I'm not going to dispute Your game plan. No way!

The Dublin images continue to haunt me. However, I still have to put up the tree, do my Christmas shopping, and go through the copy editing of the book. Nonetheless, forming those images in metaphor should start tomorrow. One metaphor a day ought to do it. I must "see things," if not anything like the way Seamus Heaney does, at least in some fashion, for my own spiritual welfare if for nothing else. Why do I always arrange my life so there are things happening — Thanksgiving this time — when I come back from a long plane flight?

And I have the trip to Boston next week — and every supper till Christmas already filled.

Help me to realize that Advent starts Sunday!

I love You.

November 28, 1991, Thanksgiving — Grand Beach

My Love,

Late in the afternoon, the house swarming with relatives and friends, me tired from the jet lag and disoriented. And the Bears lost! The Mass was nice. It was good to see a lot of the old faces again.

I am in no mood for prayer. I've come up to my room to escape the noise and the chaos and I'll try to come back later on, though You know how often I do that.

However, to get down to brass tacks so to speak, this year has been one of the most astonishing in my life, a lot of old lost battles suddenly won, a world turned topsy-turvy. As I was saying to Marilyn at the opera last night, all I need now for perfection is either a novel that catches fire, or better, a movie adaptation — and Governor Mario as president!

For none of these do I ask, unless they please You, and then of course I'll gladly accept them!

There is still time in the world for wonder and surprise, for events that are pure grace, mind-boggling events, which tell me something about myself and about You.

I am grateful for them, for all Your blessings, from my father on down to little Neil Thomas, the new grandnephew, and all the good and wonderful things which have made my life so exciting. I don't deserve any of them, and I don't lay claim to any of them as a matter of right, but I am very grateful indeed and I love You very much. However many years are left to me, help me to respond well to all the invitations You offer to me.

November 29, 1991 — Grand Beach

My Love,

I'm beginning to come down to earth after the trip and I'm back on a regular spiritual reading basis — Louis MacNeice, the Irish Protestant poet (who writes often much like an Irish Catholic), and Cardinal Martini on the church.

I've also read this morning Walt Connor's *The Accidental Proletariat*, a fascinating and threatening book about the USSR. What will happen in the remnants of that inept empire? It is hard to believe that an empire of which we were frightened five years ago disappeared overnight last summer, creating a huge vacuum in the world. I forgot among my things to be grateful for yesterday the end of that empire and the evil Party which dominated it. I also want to pray for the people of what used to be the USSR and for the new nations that are emerging from it. I fear they will have to pay a terrible price in suffering in years to come for the terrible ideology that enveloped that vast area for seventy years. I wish I had more confidence in our leadership's ability to respond sensitively to the situation.

MacNeice has a lovely poem about the sound of a railroad train at night when he was young, how soothing and reassuring it was. I know the exact feeling. I have experienced it many times here at Grand Beach in the summer time, but that experience also recalls something much deeper in my own past. I would not have heard the train on Augusta Boulevard or Mayfield Avenue, so it must go back to my earliest years on Austin Boulevard before I was six years old. But the experience was the same as his — the soft rumble waking me in the night and the feeling that somehow I was reassured by the sound, perhaps by the presence of the outside world beyond my dreams, perhaps also by my romantic identification with trains as the gateway to adventure. Anyway trains and train noises are a sacrament to me, a sign of grace and transcendent presence in the world, this time in benign sounds and power and a hint of adventure. A love sign of Your presence in the world.

Martini talks about the church as mystery, as Your presence in the world. Surely it is all of that and I believe in it totally. Unfortunately the institution, in its present form, defaces that mystery. It does not obscure it completely and much of what the institution says is valid and important. But self-righteousness and power hunger and insensitivity and hypocrisy have deprived it of most of its credibility. Is it too much to hope that You who have accomplished so many wonders both in the world and in my own personal life during the past year can also somehow change the face of the institutional church?

Anyway I thank You once again for all Your blessings and graces and ask You to help me make the most of the busy Advent season ahead of me. I love You.

November 30, 1991 — Grand Beach

My Love,

I read Robertson Davies's new novel yesterday, about "Murther." It's a marvelous book, a *tour de force* about a man who is able to see, in purgatory perhaps, films of the lives of his ancestors back to the revolutionary war. I wish I had more knowledge of my progenitors. There's only a few pictures and some memory of stories, none of which go beyond the grandparent level. A lot of tragedy, a lot of early death, a lot of wasted lives.

We are blessed that the lot of humankind has improved so dramatically. I am blessed that my life has been so much better than that of any imaginable ancestor. I thank You for them and for the faith and courage without which I would not have come to exist. I wonder if sometime I ought to try to create a story about these predecessors I don't know. I'm tempted to say that they were probably peasants for generations and nothing interesting ever happened to them. Nothing, that is, except everything that matters — life, love, marriage, children, death. It would be a fascinating exercise to try to imagine them and thus perhaps to pay my debt of gratitude that their lives and loves made me possible, and my debt of gratitude to You for enabling me to stand on the shoulders of giants! For all those who came before us are giants!

Martini says this morning that the creation groans, we groan, the Spirit groans (following St. Paul of course). We all groan for unity. The most interesting part of it — and the most challenging — is that the Spirit groans. YOU groan. Dare I say You do so as a woman in the advanced state of arousal groans for her husband to fulfill his love for her? I don't doubt the validity of that metaphor. Your yearning for our love led to the emptying of Yourself in the Incarnation. That You yearn for us is a truth that is so overwhelming that I find it hard to remember and even harder to absorb.

Yet that's what life is all about. I stand on the shoulders of the giants because You yearn for me. I must hear Your yearning in all the sounds of the world, like the train about which I reflected yesterday and the wind which roars off the lake this morning. All sacraments of Your Love.

Help me to continue to listen for You.

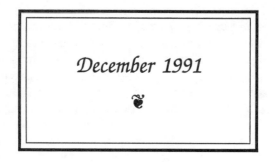

December 1991

December 1, 1991 — Grand Beach

My Love,

Just when I'm thinking of ancestors because of the Davies book, I see Eileen Durkin's work on our family tree program and realize that my grandfather was born the year after the famine of one John Greeley and Peggy Cunane. I wonder who these two people really were? How did they manage to survive the famine, marry, and have children. Even beyond the definition, they must have been giants. How much I would like to know more about them, who they were, how they lived, how they died. I do know — and perhaps it's all I need to know — that they were people of faith and courage and love.

I also read yesterday Kate O'Brien's *The Last of Summer,* a book about 1939 and the doomed young men and women who were about to be swept up in Hitler's war. It was tragic reading as we draw near to the fiftieth anniversary of Pearl Harbor.

They would have died anyway. We all die anyway. I remember the argument I had with someone who said that it was unjust for people to die without a life, as though that compounded the original injustice of death itself and as if that somehow was an argument against You. Such folk seem to think that anger at You is an argument against You.

It is all mystery, of course. You are mystery. My existence is mystery. Life is a mystery. Anything at all is a mystery. We understand no better now than did my ancestors in County Mayo or the first reflecting creatures that came out of the forests why there is anything at all. Mystery! Mystery! Mystery!

But anyway, You are the only possible explanation of mystery. Therefore this Thanksgiving weekend as I prepare to drive back to Chicago, I give thanks for Peggy and John and for life and for anything and everything and for You. I try, however bootlessly, to join with their sufferings and their hopes and expect that someday we will all meet again in the city of Your love.

December 2, 1991 — Chicago

My Love,

It's the poet's mission to see transcendence everywhere, to hear the rumors of angels as they flap their massive wings, to sniff the aroma of Your presence wherever they go. Poets, indeed all artists, are sacrament-makers. I reflect on this as I ponder Mac-Neice's poems and the end of Buechner's book, both pretty grim and Protestant in their view of the world and life, but still aware, painfully aware, of the presence of grace.

So it seems to me, the priest by definition is almost a poet, also a sacrament-maker, a man who points to the presence of grace. But to do so with the greatest effectiveness, he must also be a seer, a man who sees grace at work in the world, as do all poets and artists worthy of the name.

As I walk through the streets of the city today and tomorrow, walking in part because they've shut down the pool here for a couple of weeks, which is all I need, I will see in this Advent time special signs of grace everywhere — windows, trees, lights, kids — and I will hear the music of Christmas and smell the scent of Christmas and as I wrap the presents feel the touch of Christmas.

My tree is up (after the usual difficulties I have with such things), the cribs are in place, the candles for Christmas and Hanukkah are ready, the pine smell is in the air. All the sensory reminders of the celebration that I need. Now the trick is to permit these sacraments of Love to seduce me into remembrance, to recall the event and the mysteries and Mystery which lie behind it.

In a certain sense all these sacraments are artificial. An angel might not need them (though my angel Gabriella would love them). But human that I am, with the limitations of my physical body, I need them (and like herself I love them). I am grateful for so many signs of wonder all about me. Help me to revel in them this Advent time so I can better reveal Mystery, i.e., You!

December 4, 1991 — Chicago

My Love,

I'm at O'Hare on the plane getting ready to take off for Boston.

I still can't grasp how quickly I've moved from being a total outsider to being an insider with influence. I must be very cautious and restrained in my use of this influence, both to conserve it and not to abuse it. I think this means that I must be reluctant to intervene unless asked. Reluctant doesn't mean I won't; rather it means that I will do so only for the most powerful reasons. Guide my instincts in this matter.

In his poems for today, MacNeice pleads to escape from the poetic impulse. He wants to be free from the imperative to see in things more than the things themselves. Can't a train just be a train? Why does it have to be a demanding metaphor? It is a cry to see the world as mundane, as pointing to nothing beyond itself. All of us are to some extent mundane — I am myself very mundane at this moment in this aluminum tube. But none of us can be entirely mundane. We are all poets, all sacrament-makers, all pilgrims of the wonderful, all entranced by the Mystery that lurks inside of and beyond and in back of and in front of all things. Despite ourselves, we are explorers of the mysterious. What if there isn't any Mystery there? Then of course we've been cheated by Reality. But as soon as one says that, one has fallen into the trap of admitting Reality and we're back to the game. Logic and poetry combined point to You.

Thank You again for the astonishingly mysterious course of my recent life.

December 5, 1991 — Boston

My Love,

My supper with the Ryans and the Connors was great fun. They are very witty, bright, and committed people. And they understand what my novels are about, which is so gratifying. It would be very nice if You, having straightened out my relationship with the archdiocese and the university, would now somehow straighten out the image of my novels, so that people can really see that they're about You and all the chances and the second chances You provide in our lives.

I realize that's a big order and of course it is a self-serving request. It's up to You. You move me to write the stories. Their success is Your work. If You want them to be truly understood by those who have not read them, it's up to You.

When I ask for this, I do not want to seem any less grateful for all the good things You've showered on me all my life, especially in the last year.

I am grateful for everything. I love You.

December 6, 1991 — Boston

My Love,

I'm at Logan Airport waiting for the plane back to Chicago. Tired and confused and determined to lose money, gloves, hat, and scarf. I've been bungling around for the last twenty-four hours. I hope I don't mess up any worse before I get home.

Evey Riesman has Alzheimer's and is clearly dying. David, who is close to eighty, now shows his years. Yet he still looks at her with love. That look alone is enough to justify the trip and make it a blessing and a grace.

Also the others, Orlando happy (and deservedly) over his National Book Award and fascinated by St. Paul (and ready to become a Catholic); his Celtic wife, beautiful, bright, and also ready to be a Catholic if the church would only ordain women and change on birth control; Jim and Jean, happy together; Kevin and Marilyn uneasy about whether they have been the kind of Catholics they should be (and of course they are and have been);

the Connors, funny, funny, funny, and also dedicated — grace abounding all around me, for which I am very grateful indeed.

I've talked myself into this trip. I have a special role to play and I must continue to play it while there's yet time.

I'll be tired and irritable when I get home and have to make phone calls.

I love You.

December 7, 1991 — Grand Beach

Pearl Harbor Day. Fifty years ago. Bears being bombed by the Cardinals. Interruption to announce attack. Fires on *Oklahoma*. Back to game. McAfee touchdown, Bears ahead! As clear as yesterday.

Can it be fifty years? Can so much have happened? Are those old men on TV who talk about the attack near-contemporaries of mine? I don't feel that old. I don't even look that old. But I am that old. Not much time left, is there?

Anyway, I pray for all those who died in the war, including especially the twenty-two from St. Angela parish — that many! It didn't seem like a lot then, but I was too young to understand the tragedy of each death. And there were forty million at least!

May there never be another such again.

I'm also grateful for all that has happened in my life in that half century. I have been blessed indeed, beyond my wildest expectations. Thank You for everything.

December 8, 1991 — Grand Beach

My Love,

Mariette in Ecstasy is the novel of an upstate New York order of French Canadian nuns and a seventeen-year-old stigmatic postulant. Eventually she is thrown out of the community because the "miracle" of her stigmata is disturbing the community. The author leaves us in doubt whether she is a faker, crazy, or a saint. It's another one of those "Agnes of God" things about nuns where you are left in doubt, a tricky and perhaps unsatisfying ending, but very well written.

It brought many memories of the seminary and the spirituality we were taught there, one that has dominated the religious life for a long time. It's pretty well rejected now even by the Jesuits who imposed it on us in the seminary. I wonder if much of what went wrong in religious life after the Council came from that spirituality of what we would now call repression. Or perhaps a mix of formation in that spirituality and then the new pop psychological one which replaced it. Was the baby thrown out with the bathwater? Was there any truth at all in that grim, rigid, oppressive spirituality? Was that the way You wanted to be served?

In truth I doubt it, but You still loved those who served You in it and their efforts at generosity and dedication. Moreover one cannot accept (this one can't anyway) the notion that saints from Benedict to Teresa and Ignatius were completely wrong. However, they were religious, and their spirituality needed adjustment to be applied to secular priests, to say nothing of the laity. We are not monks and nuns *manqués*. But what can we take from their tradition, at its best, and use in a spirituality for today and tomorrow?

I don't think we've even begun, and I doubt that the current political and environmental spiritualities are even a good beginning because both lack what the religious orders had if they had anything at all — a sense of the transcendent.

Do the Irish have the secret? A spirituality of sacramentalism? Even in Joyce?

Perhaps. I'll have to think more on this, though I doubt that I'm the one to try to do it.

December 9, 1991 — Grand Beach

My Love,

I am grateful for the pleasant and relaxing weekend here, only one phone call for two days. It's a nice way to get ready for the chaos of the next two weeks. I hope that in the crazy days ahead I can keep some sense of what Christmas is about. Help me to listen to the music, see the lights, reflect on the story. I know I won't do it perfectly but grant me the grace to immerse myself in Christmas despite the rushing and running and the ill tempers.

I mean immerse myself on the level of poetry, of image and story and picture. I guess that means I have to write some Christmas poetry too, maybe as part of these reflections. I'll try in the days ahead to turn this reflection into a poetic exercise.

So at this time of light and darkness I'll be closer to You.

December 11, 1991 — Chicago

CHRISTMAS HAIKU

Myriad white lights
On Michigan Avenue
Magnificent mile

December 12, 1991 — Chicago

Warm December wind
Anxious shoppers crowd the mall
Cloudless sapphire sky

December 13, 1991 — Chicago

Rain soaks the flutist
Hoping for a dollar bill
He plays "Silent Night"

Golden cocktail dress
Bare shouldered women, short skirts
Christmas party time

December 14, 1991 — Chicago

My Love,

Despite the sunshine and a good talk with the cardinal last night, I am feeling depressed. All the sickness in my friends. The

Irish prayer to remind us that we are dying. MacNeice's grim poetry — not much Christmas joy in that despite the bright light of the sun, the soft candles, the smell of pine, and the fragrant poinsettias.

I will die. I may die painfully. I may die alone — these are the thoughts that trouble me as I rush through life. A wedding today, a wedding tomorrow. Vitality and decline. Love and death.

> A flickering flame
> Wind rattles my windows
> Red poinsettia leaves

December 16, 1991 — Chicago

My Love,

I'm troubled by how I performed the Phelan wedding. Everyone seemed very pleased with the story about the strawberries and the tone of joy and laughter with which I conducted the services. But I wonder if I diverted attention from the bride and groom to myself.

Was it *too* skilled a performance? I'm not sure and there's no real way to find out. Should I have somehow made it less a fun occasion and hence call less attention to myself? Obviously not, but where is the line drawn? Where in my plans for the ceremony did I begin to engage in self-display, if I did?

Same for the Mass at Saint Mary of the Woods in the morning. The people like my style, but does my style get in the way of You?

I hope not, but I'm not sure how I'll ever know or how I'll be able to decide.

December 17, 1991 — Chicago

My Love,

> Tinsel red and gold
> Low-slung sun, deep sapphire sky
> Handel violins

December 19, 1991 — Tampa Airport

My Love,

I'm sorry I missed yesterday. I thought I'd have a couple of hours in the hotel room — and a chance to swim — but the schedule changed. I came here as a favor. I also found out that I was supposed to give the graduation address, a complete surprise. Fortunately I got away with telling the St. Brigid story, but what if I didn't have a repertory of stories? The graduation itself was chaos, kids and parents streaming out as soon as their names were mentioned — eighteen hundred names! A fair number didn't listen to the story — they didn't listen to anything. An exercise in futility. Right now I'm a wreck, a tired, old wreck with stuffed sinuses.

Sorry to complain, but as I've said before I believe that like any lover You want to hear even my complaints. Help Jack and Marvin, I beg You.

December 20, 1991 — Chicago

My Love,

> Plain song melodies
> Singing of Mother Mary
> In faint winter light

December 21, 1991 — Chicago

My Love,

> Chocolate everywhere
> And cookies, candies, shortbread —
> Christmas calories!

December 22, 1991 — Chicago

My Love,

Coming down the home stretch at Christmas and despite all the music and the lights and the flowers I'm still weary. No one thinks I'm tired and discouraged, so I guess I keep up a good act. I wonder. Is my problem faith? Has my heart truly been hardened by all the work I do, all the responsibilities I have taken upon myself? There is nothing wrong with work, nor with responsibilities, but if they take the "something extra" out of life, then there is something wrong with me.

I read MacNeice's poems about England before the war when death was closing in from all sides, and I realize that I'm living in a magical era of good news (save in the church) and wonder why I am not happier — especially at Christmas time. Especially since in my crowded and complex life there is more good news than bad.

Help me the next couple of days to get back on the track of joy.

> Thick fog curls outside
> Cutting me off from the world —
> Music box carols

December 23, 1991 — Chicago

> Mysterious night
> Bewitching mists and white lights —
> Winter's victory

My Love,

In the reading from Cardinal Martini for today, he speaks of Martha and Mary and enters shrewdly and sympathetically into the psychology of both. He does not drift off into nonsense, comparing the contemplative and active lives, but rather observes that listening and loving *is* the better part of human life even if the activity is always necessary.

I am truly Martha, busy about many things this Christmas time and finding most of them flat and empty and frustrating, the cultural events and the parties and dinners and lunches I go to.

It is necessary that I go to these things, necessary that I be pleasant and happy and charming, even though I feel hollow inside. But it is the hectic rush of such events which in part makes me feel hollow because I do not have time to relax and reflect and absorb the wonders of the season. Despite the poems I have written, the imagery that courses through my head, I feel barren, empty.

Today is a perfect example. I would like to spend the day in prayer and reflection. But I have obligations to fulfill. And the cleaning person is here in the apartment, which makes reflection impossible.

How do I balance Martha and Mary? Cardinal Martini offers no magic solution. And I haven't been able to find one myself despite decades of trying. But I surely am busy about many things and I know in my heart that only one thing is necessary.

Yet I do believe, and I am grateful, and I do Love.

December 24, 1991 — Chicago

My Love,

> Sparkling saffron lights
> The city glows at midnight
> Quiet Christmas Eve

December 25, 1991 — Chicago

> Cloudless Christmas sky
> The city brown and still —
> Sunlight washes the earth

Merry Christmas my Love!

December 26, 1991 — Chicago

My Love,

Kind of late to be reflecting, but I woke up this morning and continued to work on my abortion research and got carried away by it. I hope to finish it tomorrow as I fly up to Madison and back to visit Clete [Bishop Cletus O'Donnell]. I dread the plane flight but loyalty and friendship demand that I make the trip.

Grant that I may bring a little joy into his life as he goes through this illness. I pray for him and for everyone who suffers in any way.

December 28, 1991 — Chicago

My Love,

The trip to Madison yesterday was a gloomy experience, as I knew it would be. The bishop does not look his seventy-four years. He is still a tall, broad-shouldered, handsome man, more like a bishop than any bishop I know. But he is a shell of his former self because of the stroke. Able to walk and talk, but with difficulty, caught inside a body which no longer responds to his mind. What a terrible fate!

He is a great churchman, one who if the church was run with any intelligence today would be in some place much bigger than Madison (as would many other competent bishops). Even with the stroke he is notably above the mean on intelligence and ability. There is tragedy for him and for the church in this situation.

But quite apart from that tragedy is the personal tragedy of the stroke, much worse because he is not fully alive and never will be again.

That could happen to me, I tell myself. Or some other equally humiliating, painful, and destructive form of slow death. Most likely something of the sort will happen to me. That is inevitably a depressing thought. I accept whatever form of death You intend for me but I also fear it. The only choice is to trust in You and take what comes as bravely as I can.

So much sickness among so many dear friends! It seems as if I'm spending all my time visiting the sick. Well, not quite, but it does dishearten me. Sickness and old age are part of being human. One must accept them as a condition for the human condition. Accept, accept, accept... that is the only word I have this morning to describe how I feel these days. But it is a valid word for my state of mind, especially if I add the adverb "fearfully."

However, one must go on living, must continue one's responsibilities, and even celebrate the life that remains.

And I must be grateful for all the good things that have happened to me during my life.

Grant that in whatever time is left I may come to know You better.

December 30, 1991 — Chicago

My Love,

If love exists — and there can be no doubt at this time of the year that it does — then Love must exist. Here is the heart of mystery. Or Mystery. How can there be thought without Thought? How can there be love without Love? How can there be attraction without Attraction? How can there be happiness without Happiness? How can there be fun without Fun? If there is anything at all, than there must be Something/Someone, must there not? Anything else would be even more of a mystery!

Take care of all my friends who are suffering, I beg You, and please deepen my faith and my courage and my trust in You.

December 31, 1991 — Chicago

My Love,

The last day of an eventful year both in the world and in my own life. I want to thank You for all the blessings of the year, for my family, my friends, those who love me and whom I love, the various reconciliations in my life, my health, the prospering of my work, and all other good things with which You have showered me.

I am especially grateful for the reconciliation with the cardinal (and my almost immediate opportunity to be helpful to the church in Chicago) and for my new relationship with the university. Neither is perfect, but they are more than I had expected and both are mystery and grace in my life.

Thank You with all my heart.

The dark sign during the year has been the illness of others, so much sickness, so much suffering, so much worry. All I can do today while I thank You for my own health is to pray for the health of all the others and ask for the continuation of my own health as long as it is part of Your plan. And the strength to cope with aging and weakening.

Help me during the year which starts tomorrow to continue to serve You and to know You better and love You better.

January 1992

January 1, 1992 — Chicago

My Love,

I thank You for bringing me to the beginning of 1992, and I ask You to take care of me and protect me during the new year and continue to love and bless me.

I know that Your love is unshakeable, but I do believe that it is appropriate to ask that it be continued, because lovers always like to hear that their love is needed and wanted.

This is the day when people make resolutions. I have two. One is to continue vigorously to hold my weight in check; the other is to continue to work on relaxation and reflection.

Work on relaxation! How like me that sounds, but You know what I mean.

In the two months I'll be in Tucson (when I'm not traveling around on planes) I'll have only to begin work on a new novel, learn Word for Windows and Windows on the computer, and attend to correspondence and phone calls. That's not a large agenda. Grant that I can stick to it and come back here in mid-March refreshed and relaxed and ready for the spring quarter in the class room at the University of Chicago.

I spent the morning cleaning out all the food I was given for Christmas. It's a shame to throw out food, but what else can be done with so much chocolate. That also represents a new beginning, a fresh start.

Yes, my Love, that's what today is, a new beginning, and for that blessing the fireworks at the lake front last night were an appropriate activity.

I love You.

January 2, 1992 — Chicago

My Love,

In Martini's new book, which I began this morning, he notes that the Spirit, Your Spirit, prays within us. Our prayers are spirit-driven. I believe that You do pray within me, even when I'm tired like I am this morning, that Your Spirit speaks to my spirit so I can speak back to You. Just now that's enough to give me hope when I am as utterly flat as I am today.

I do love You. Help me to love You more.

January 3, 1992 — Chicago

> Rockets at midnight
> Silver flowers in the fog
> Welcome the new year

My Love,

That haiku has been lurking in my head since New Year's. I wanted to get it down. It's the last of my Christmas poems. No, come to think of it, there'll be one for Twelfth Night too.

I read Martini on prayer this morning and realized that I am not a natural prayer. I do not have a reflective and contemplative personality. I need all kinds of artificial helps to pray and, despite life-long efforts, haven't become very good at it.

The most important grace in my prayer life has been this practice of daily, journal-like reflections. It's been an enormous help, and for that I'm very grateful. But I reflected as I read Martini that I neither pray before I do this nor after I'm finished. Rather I rush into it and rush out of it. Moreover, I need artificial markers to wrench myself away from the rest of the day to think about You and Your Love.

Some lover!

On the one hand, You made me what I am and You love me as I am. On the other hand I can do better, with Your help!

Therefore, I resolve to pray on my knees both before and after these reflections (when I'm not in an airplane!). Help me to keep this resolution.

January 5, 1992 — Chicago

My Love,

At Mass yesterday I told the story of Babuska, the woman who was host for the Wise Men their last night in Bethlehem. People loved it of course because it is a wonderful story. The warning for us in the story is that like Babuska we are so busy with the many obligations and responsibilities of life that we have no time to visit the Young King.

You, in other words.

In these days after Christmas I have been on the run, discharging final obligations and getting ready for the transition to Tucson.

I've not had time for You. Well, that's not true, but what is true is that my life has been too frantic to have enough time for You. Like I say, some lover, huh?

So I've fallen victim to Babuska's faults. You still pray within me. You still love me. I ought not to give up. But as I look back on a frantic and exciting life I have many regrets, and that is the biggest. Since the very first day at Christ the King parish almost thirty eight years ago, I have been on the run.

I hope it isn't too late to slow down a little and live a more prayerful and reflective life. I will always be busy and involved as long as You give me life and health (and again for yesterday's good report, much thanks). But can't I be that way and be more prayerful too?

At least a little bit more prayerful?

Help me, my Love, to make some progress during the Tucson interlude.

January 6, 1992 — Chicago

My Love,

The Epiphany party yesterday was great fun. It's hard to leave for Tucson after spending time with so many people who love me. How good You have been to me to surround me with so many people who are sacraments of Your love.

I love You.

January 7, 1992 — Tucson

My Love,

I've begun to read the first year of reflections since I began this journal, and it is an interesting and disturbing experience. Interesting because I see myself in a mirror even sharper than that of my autobiography. Disturbing because my problems haven't changed much and I haven't changed much. I'm also reading Madeleine L'Engle's journal, which makes mine look pathetic.

We'll see as time goes on who the person is who talks to You in this journal. I'm not sure I like him all that much, though he does have an agile mind and a glib tongue. The point is that You love him, so he can't be all bad.

Martini has a great line this morning about prayer. We begin, he says, by saying "O Lord, I am not able to pray! But if You want me to try, then You must pray within me."

I can buy that. How many times again today have I dashed away from this screen to take care of things that I've remembered must be done in the transition to a new place and a slightly new life.

I really can't pray very well, but it is presumptuous, isn't it, to think that I could or should? The only reason I dare to address You in prayer, much less the intimate form of prayer which at least sometimes this journal involves, is that You want me to pray. Indeed, unless I misunderstand You, You say that You need me to pray.

So I try and I rely on the help of Your spirit to even begin, much less to remember through the day that You care for me far more than I could possibly care for You. I'll keep trying.

January 8, 1992 — Tucson

My Love,

I saw the movie *Blackrobe* last night — about early missionaries in America — and it gave me much to think about. I had read the story somewhere, and the film made me remember some of the incidents.

I had more than my fill of Jesuit missionary martyrs in the seminary. The Jesuit propaganda turned me off. Now when I see the film I am astonished again at the bravery of those men and also their arrogance (ditto for St. Francis Xavier). The bravery was deliberate, the arrogance was not. But today we see that baptizing people so they can get into heaven is questioning the universality of Your love. Moreover, while some of the indigenous people were cruel and superstitious pagans, was the missionary conviction about water-saving any less than superstitious? Was not the Inquisition at least as cruel? Are not we today equally barbaric in our wars (140,000 killed in Iraq is the latest estimate)?

I've seen the emergence of this new attitude towards mission in my lifetime, a revolution in the church's thinking about itself and its mission. The Jesuits in the seminary, with an arrogance perhaps less understandable than that of the missionary martyrs, bought the same simplistic notions of salvation, of Your merciful love, and of the superiority of Western culture. Indeed some of the babble about evangelization is not all that different, like the pope's notion that Europe is to be re-Christianized from the Atlantic to the Urals. Not by the crowd in charge these days, that's for sure!

Where does that leave us? I'm not sure I know or that I have to know. Obviously we must respect and absorb into our approach the best in every culture. Obviously those who become Catholic bring their heritage along with them. Just as obviously, it seems to me, we must not become cultural relativists; we must not believe that one culture is as good as another or that one religion is as good as another.

Not much of this impinges directly on my life, but I'm going to have to write a column on this subject, one that asks how the church can truly appeal to people without imposing either superstition or cultural alienation on them.

Well, a lot of idea stuff tonight, but I had to work this out in my own head.

I love You.

January 9, 1992 — Tucson

My Love,

To continue last night's reflections on *Black Robe:* The weakness of the black robes and all "evangelizers" is that they are unable to trust enough in Your love. They are going to have a program, a plan, a process — whether it be the RCIA [Rite of Christian Initiation of Adults] or mass baptisms — which will mold others into Catholics by force. There is no room in their plans for Your love or for the prompting of Your Spirit. The opposite extreme is not to do anything at all, which might be my temptation because I'm so turned off by all programs and programmers. Somewhere in between is an approach in persuasion and freedom, but it's not easy to figure out what that is. But at least we must not shortchange either Your love or the Spirit's ability to move wherever She will.

The crucial question one must ask is what kind of image of You underlies the strategy. Here *Blackrobe* missed the point entirely. You were the kind of God who would deny happiness to a noble Indian because the water ceremony had not been performed. Such an attitude would be intolerable now, but it was intolerable even then, though they perhaps had more excuse.

Need I reflect on these matters? Only if I tend to make the church more important than You, which is a temptation to which we are all subject. Increasingly I think I am going in the opposite direction, especially with my contempt for the way the priesthood behaves. The other extreme is to think that Catholicism doesn't matter at all.

But it does! In its essence it says that You're catholic! Your saving love covers everyone and everything that is groaning for salvation! But because we believe that, we should be more relaxed and confident in our efforts to cooperate with Your work — and in my case perhaps less depressed about the way our leaders are currently fouling up.

Tomorrow I'll reflect on *Madame Bovary*, another film that fascinated me.

January 10, 1992 — Tucson

My Love,

Madame Bovary as a film seems even more cruel than it did as a novel. Flaubert has nothing but contempt for Emma, a particularly nasty and mean French contempt. He is a kind of vengeful fundamentalist god to his creature. He feels not the slightest bit of affection for her, poor, romantic daydreamer that she is. Rather he is icy, superior, snobbish. Yeah, the book is a classic, but a vicious classic. I could never treat one of my characters that way, especially not to enhance my own feelings of superiority.

If the storyteller is a metaphor for God, Flaubert is a negative metaphor. He reveals what You are *not*. Bad things happen in life to good people, to shallow romantics, and to everyone else. But You don't delight in their suffering; rather You suffer with us. You suffered with Emma in the story and will with others who are disappointed by the poor match between their romantic dreams and the boredom of life!

You also suffer with romantics like me whose dreams come true, indeed more than we ever expect, and then have to cope with the demands of such fulfilled dreams and the reality that even they can't satisfy us.

You love me more than I could even begin to dream about loving anyone else. And need me more than I could need anyone else.

January 11, 1992 — Tucson

My Love,

I'm up early this morning because I couldn't sleep last night. There's something warm and cozy about a dark morning, even when one hasn't slept enough and even when one is alone.

Because, of course, one isn't alone. You're here — in the warmth of the house, in the soft sound of WFMT, in the comforting lamps, in the stars and the desert, so quiet, outside. You're present in all of them with Your peace and love.

I should be more aware of that presence; it is so easy to notice it when one stops for only a moment. L'Engle this morning reflects on the oak tree. She says that the oak must be terrifying if you don't believe in God because of it "isness." Well, yes, because being is terrifying if you think of it as mindless and irrational. Being is either that way or it is love. Or, better, Love.

Love everywhere if only we had the wisdom to see it — *You*.

When I take time to read poetry or find a good spiritual book, I see these things instantly and even remember them a little while. But I still need enormous help from You to pull back even a few moments from my almost pathological preoccupations and notice the splendor of being, of You.

I've been looking back at reading my own reflections. They're not as elegant as L'Engle's. But I am surprised by them, by the depth and the wisdom and the honesty that is there, as the reviewer in the *Tablet* said. I somehow feel that the man who wrote these pages is not me. Or not me the way I ordinarily live.

Help me, my Beloved, to live up to the wisdom I learn from all the sacraments, human and non-human, with which You have surrounded me.

January 12, 1992 — Tucson

My Love,

A cold cloudy Sunday morning today with a hint of clearing and sun — how like the church in Chicago! I'm grateful that I've been able to live to see the changes, that perhaps I have made some contribution to them, and that the future may enable me to make more. I've been waiting twenty-seven years for this opportunity and I am very happy about it. Now if only the rest of the church would wake up and return to the days of good Pope John.

O Lady Love, You who preside over the sun and the clouds, the cold and the warm, and who has guided me through the joys and sorrows of life, help me to have confidence in the warmth and the sun as hints of the world to come and also as suggestions of Your curious but effective ways of working in the world. Help me never to lose hope in Your love and Your wisdom and Your plans. I ask this through Jesus the Lord.

January 13, 1992 — Tucson

My Love,
    I watched *Mr. and Mrs. Bridge* on TV last night. I suppose that if one wants to reduce to prose the explanation for the meaning of life contained in the story it is that a silly woman and a rigid man lost wonderful opportunities to develop the love they actually felt towards one another. It's a story which could apply to many marriages and human relationships — fear of risk-taking standing in the way of love. Paul Newman and Joanne Woodward played the roles perfectly, did they not? One of the weaknesses of the film was that its milieu — Kansas City during the thirties — might enable viewers to avoid applying the story to themselves. The background, however, reminded me of my parents, whose marriage I knew in approximately the same era and who suffered from some of the same inability to communicate with one another about love and hence missed glorious chances for the expression of love.
    A celibate is not faced with that risk — which is no reason for being a celibate, is it?
    I marvel at the differences among humans and how we all have spontaneous ambivalent reactions towards the other. The trick is to resist taking these reactions seriously and making them the basis for a political or personal program. How much better if we would enjoy and revel in the diversity You have created instead of trying to put it down (as husbands and wives often do). We ought to enjoy one another instead of being offended by difference.
    At the Notre Dame–UCLA game on Saturday there were two young and very obnoxious Bruin fans behind me. I must admit that in the excitement of the game I felt like slugging them or saying something nasty. It would have been foolish, especially since they ended our seventy-game streak! Afterwards I realized that all I really had against them (in addition to their loud voices!) was the fact that they took something that was not serious very seri-

ously indeed, which is to say more seriously than I did. I should have enjoyed their misguided enthusiasm!

O Lord, who has made me a mix of spirit and matter, help the joy in my body influence joy in my soul and the joy in my soul to animate my body so that as a truly happy person I might lead others to know You better and celebrate Your grace more fully. I ask this in the name of Jesus the Lord.

Amen.

January 14, 1992 — Tucson

My Love,

Franz Joseph Haydn playing in the background, lovely music for this hour in the morning. Thank You for the sacrament of love.

Words are on my mind this morning. Keith Wilson talks about the fragility of everything, including the poems he writes. L'Engle agonizes about why she is putting words on paper for her journal. Her only answer is that she has to do so. Indeed she is awakened in the middle of the night by her journal and the need to continue to write. Martini talks about words of joy in Mary's prayers. And I continue to read my own journal, astonished at what is in it and how much I have forgotten.

I'm not a writer. I have never been able to think of myself as a writer and I still can't despite the output. I am a priest who writes and I write for priestly purposes.

It's part of my ministry to the wonders of my mail-box parish. Help me never to forget that. I could not be like the Irish priest who is on leave of absence from his diocese so he can write. Writing for me is quintessentially priestly work. Hence I can afford to make it my identity.

O God, who has given me a gift of words and storytelling, grant that I may always use that gift for Your service in love and fidelity and joy and that my witness may always bring others closer to You. I ask this in the name of Jesus the Lord.

Amen.

January 15, 1992 — Tucson

My Love,

It's a bitter cold morning, but the sun is out. However, back in Chicago the winds are forty miles an hour; there's a blizzard going on and four inches of snow. I thank You this morning for the gift of this Arizona assignment during the last thirteen years (can it have been that long?) which has protected me from that kind of winter. Brr! Mind you, I never planned a place like this and would not mind terribly if I had to return to Chicago winters because I like Chicago so much. On the other hand it's nice to return to a place You love and the gift of coming here is a surprise, a gift indeed, a grace.

Lawrence Kasdan's film *Grand Canyon,* which I saw last night, is about grace. He observes both grace and random violence in Los Angeles and wonders which makes sense — miracles or "shit." The answer is the Grand Canyon, which stands for timelessness and beauty and majesty and is in the film (as well as in reality) a symbol, a metaphor, a *sacrament of You.* A somewhat hesitant sacrament because Kasdan is not sure about You (but then who is as sure as a catechism teacher?), but a sacrament nonetheless.

"Sometimes," the Kevin Kline character says, "things work out." Sometimes they don't, but grace abounds in the story nonetheless, even if some of the characters turn their backs on it and other characters' conversion to grace is uncertain. But then that's the way the world is.

The film's merit is that it is about the mystery of grace. It confronts head-on the mystery of evil with the mystery of grace. How is it that both exist? What can one do in a world where "grace" and "shit" co-exist? One can be sensitive to grace and seize all the opportunities it represents — that's Kasdan's answer and it is not a bad one.

O Lady Wisdom, Mother of Grace, Mother of Mercy, help me to open to Your Spirit wherever You blow and to respond quickly and "gracefully" to the opportunities for goodness and love which You offer to me in my life. I ask this in the name of Jesus the Lord. Amen.

January 16, 1992 — Tucson

My Love,

One of the minor themes in *Grand Canyon* is the risk in trying to help others. Sometimes it works and sometimes it doesn't. Sometimes you help people and sometimes you cause harm. Sometimes they are grateful to you. Other times they hate you and blame you. Moreover, no matter how often you do it (or don't do it), you really never develop wisdom about whether or how to do it.

A priest by definition is supposed to help people. In my younger days I thought I was being very cautious, and in fact I was indiscriminate in my attempts to help. I took people at their word that they wanted my encouragement in their work and careers. Then when I encouraged them, they blamed me for forcing them to do something they didn't want to do. Now, if anything, I've gone to the other extreme and am, to put it mildly, extremely cautious about intervening in others' lives.

I can't say that either posture is right or either one is wrong. That's the problem. It's not that I don't want to help — after all that's why I became a priest. Nor can I say I don't want to respect their freedom. I've tried to do that from the very beginning. The problem is that some people will never forgive you for helping them. So now I'm more cautious. But that's not because I've learned anything. I still can't tell when I should intervene in people's lives and when I should not. I tend to stay out, but I'm still not sure.

I'm sorry for all the mistakes I've made in the course of thirty-eight years as a priest, for the times I've intervened when I shouldn't and the times when I should have intervened and did not do so — the latter mistake being the worse of the two.

What, my Love, is the point of this reflection? I guess it is that I'll never be very good at this problem, not much better than I was at the beginning and that I'll always need Your help. I guess I also hurt from all the anger I stirred up by good intentions, especially when the good intentions were matched with skill and restraint and still distorted beyond all reasons.

I guess You understand that reaction too because You have been the target of it often Yourself. No good deed goes unpunished. People hate to feel dependent, even when there is no hidden agenda in one's help.

I remember the article by the French ex-priest who would not say the Lord's Prayer any longer because it was a prayer of dependence. He didn't like his own father and he transferred that dislike to You. Unfair? Tell me about it!

So I go on taking risks, go on being vulnerable in the act of helping, knowing that for all the experience and all the skill that comes with long practice I may still make an enemy or lose a friend or possibly both.

What else is there to do? For either of us? We must continue to try.

O vulnerable God who emptied Yourself in service of us, the way every lover gives Herself, help me to be open and courageous in my service of others, shrewd and skillful indeed, but also generous and abundant to others, just as You are. I ask this grace in the name of Jesus who emptied himself for all of us. Amen.

January 18, 1992 — Tucson

My Love,

Martini in his commentary on the Magnificat yesterday reflected on the exuberance of Mary's joy. As he says, Mary had plenty of reason to worry — the world did not look very friendly to her just then — but she chose to concentrate on the good news, the joy which was available, and ignore the rest.

Not a bad hint on how to live. This morning it's cloudy, the bad weather is apparently coming back, I have a sinus headache, I'm going through the trauma of learning two software updates, I am worried about a lot of things back home, I am growing old, I will surely die eventually, if not right now, and I can't even find a good textbook for my sociology of religion course!

So I should still be joyous?

The lesson of the Magnificat is that, yes, I should be joyous. I am alive, I have friends, I am loved.

Should I rejoice even if my life is absurd? In the *Times* yesterday a reviewer criticized Paul Davis's new book on the grounds that he ignored some of the evidence of the absurdity in the universe. Even if all is absurdity, how come there is even that? Anyway it is better to be than not to be. Or is it? Have we reason to be furious if our hunger for immortality is frustrated? Perhaps we do. But you could make a case that we're lucky to be at all. The joy we have is pure blessing and worth celebrating in itself, no matter what happens. But what about those who have so little joy? Or what about the thought that those we love will cease to be? The unacceptability of that is what finally drove William James to become a believer towards the end of his life.

I wander, my Love, from Martini's point. I do believe that my joys are hints, rumors of angels. Therefore, even when I have a sinus headache on a chilly day in Arizona, I should rejoice in all the graces in my life and particularly in grace.

I love You.

January 19, 1992 — Tucson

My Love,

A lot about kids in this morning's readings: Wilson praises a newly baptized son of one of his Mexican neighbors; Martini sees the contrast of generations in Simeon and Jesus, L'Engle wonders about the child within the self.

When, I wonder, did I become a kid freak? I'm certainly that way now, particularly during the liturgy. Was I that way at Christ the King? Perhaps, but it does not stand out in my memory. Maybe I had to have more confidence in myself before I could be at ease with kids.

When the old man holds the child in his arms, says Martini, he sees the changing of the generations, new life contrasting with his old life. He celebrates the strength of life. That vitality which we who are old admire in the young is a sacrament of Your vitality, of Your triumph of life over death. I can think that way when I "double-dip" baptize Neil Montague and Christy Durkin next week. I'll be lucky to see either of them as teenagers.

I do celebrate the life they represent — continuity, heritage, endurance, hope.

But, my Love, it is the poignancy of kids which gets to me.

The little lads and lasses who will gather around me at the altar over at Our Mother of Sorrows in a couple of hours are hope and full of hope. How easily that hope can be blighted, how easily their dreams will turn into nightmares, how much can and will go wrong in their lives.

I suppose that reaction has come from my being around the same people long enough to see how they mess up their lives — or have them messed up for them. The kids at Mass do not know much about tragedy. But they will experience it soon enough. Someday they too will be old, and that is almost automatic tragedy.

Anyway, my Love, I do believe in life. I do believe that the child is more the sacrament than the old person, though both are sacramental. I believe especially that You are ancient and new, old and child, really, as I've said before, a teenage God. The kids around me at Mass in a few hours will be sacraments of Your exuberance, Your enthusiasm, Your innocence.

And that I love. Help me to love it and understand it more.

O God, who through Jesus told us that little children are the kingdom of heaven, help me to revive my youthful enthusiasm and energy so that I too may be a sacrament of Your exuberant vitality. I ask this through the same Jesus the Lord. Amen.

January 20, 1992 — Tucson

My Love,

Martini continues to write about joy in prayer this morning as he reflects on the prayer of Jesus in St. Luke. The prayers in that gospel are, in fact, all eruptions of joy. The cardinal says that the source of the joy is wonder and surprise. There seems so little joy in my prayers. As I read the first year of this journal I encounter weariness, discouragement, resentment, but not much exuberance. How discouraging!

The most joyous part of my life now is the eucharistic celebration. At Mass all my vitality and wit and hope come to the surface, especially with kids. So there is joy within me, lots of it, joy founded in faith and excited by the wonder of the eucharistic ritual. What happens to it the rest of the time?

My paper for the NORC [National Opinion Research Center] anniversary party is about the joy of the research dance. What a contradiction! I believe in the dance and even dance in my work, but I don't dance directly with You in the morning light!

O Lord of the Dance, who wants us all to dance with You in joy, open my body and my soul to the wonder and surprise all around me and help me to come dance with You in Ireland — or any place else! Amen.

February 1992

February 4, 1992 — Chicago

My Love,

Ten days of reflections were wiped out when I mistakenly formatted my hard disk. At least they are not wiped out in Your mind.

Thanks for the good report I received from the doctor. And for the supper with the cardinal last night, which went very well. Grant that he may have the wisdom to break out of the pedophile bind before it is too late. I'm fighting a terrible group-think culture in the people around him.

Also take care of poor little Christy Durkin, whom I baptized Sunday and who is now in the hospital with a dangerous upper respiratory infection.

It's good to be back in these reflections again. I'll be back tomorrow morning on my birthday with a lot to say. I hope.

I love You.

February 5, 1992 — Chicago

My Love,

Sixty-four years drenched in grace!

It's taken me long enough to realize and even longer to begin to comprehend what that means. There is nothing in the world which is not some way or the other grace. Or grace. You lurk everywhere — sometimes, be it noted, under pretty deep disguises — waiting to envelope us/me with Your love. In the blue sky this morning and the slate gray lake, in the people on the Magnificent Mile, in the awesome skyline, in the poor and the sick and the troubled, in the friends and family who will gather with me tonight — You are *everywhere!*

I thank You for the mother and father who brought me into the world and by word and mostly example taught me about You and blessed me with the stubborn streak of independence which some people, mistakenly perhaps, call integrity. I thank You for the priesthood, which I appreciate more each year, and all the wonderfully graceful people whom I have encountered in my years in the priesthood.

I thank You for the talent with which You've blessed me and which perhaps I don't even now fully appreciate or even understand. I thank You for my health, ratified again on Monday by Dr. Phee. I thank You for the special graces of this past year, the special love, the reconciliation with the cardinal, my return to the University of Chicago. Both of these are pure grace, utterly unexpected and, to be candid, utterly undeserved. Thank You for them very much.

Thank You too for the special friends I have, people who like me and want to be with me.

I want to pray for them all, each with their own problems and challenges, especially my family (and for Baby Christy especially) and for the mayor and the cardinal.

And for Governor Mario that he run and be elected.

Again thank You very much for this happy birthday and for all the other happy birthdays through my scarcely uneventful life.

Help me in however many years I have left to grow in love in response to Your love.

February 6, 1992 — Chicago

My Love,

Yesterday was a wonderful day, like the birthdays when I was a kid that were so much fun I didn't want the day to end.

I regret being so loggy today and I am grateful for the party last night and to my family and all my friends and to You whom I love so much.

February 8, 1992 — Chicago

My Love,

Despite the joys of my birthday, I have not been very good at reflecting all this week because of the need to rush, rush, rush. There's a neat irony in all of this. I come home for celebrations and I get so worn out that the celebrations become an obligation and a responsibility.

I am now thinking seriously of returning to Tucson after the NORC anniversary for a couple of more weeks of relative peace and quiet, especially since I will have discharged all my obligations there. Praying is not easy at any time, though it is a wonderful experience. But it is almost blotted out by the endless running that is so typical of my life as I do not what I would like to do or want to do but what I have to do.

All I can say — and probably all You want me to say — is that I'll keep trying. I do love You with all my pitiful ability to love.

February 11, 1992 — Tucson

My Love,

> I praise You in the cold half moon
> Stark above the mountain
> In the wild flower
> Peeking round the rock
> In the yellow cactus fruit
> And the darting chipmunk
> In windless calm at sunrise
> And glorious crimson at the end of day
> In the royal blue sky above the desert

And in the soothing peace of blessed night
In the child's happy smile
And the old woman's glowing eyes
I praise everywhere You lurk,
Teasing me with Your love
I praise You in Mozart melodies
In the matin songs of the bustling birds
In the evensong of hungry coyote
In the rush of river waters against stone and rock
On the telephone a familiar voice
In the raindrops against my roof
In the surprise of a doorbell chime
In the implacable ticking clock
I praise You in the expressway curve
In the new terminal's sweeping arch
In the monorail's graceful bridges
In the skyline's shimmer
And the L station's walls of glass
In the dome of the old Polish church
In the white lights of the Avenue
In the quiet neighborhoods dusted with snow
In the peace of coming home.
I praise in the ingenuities of my life
The jet's hovering wings
The cheerful electric light
The VGA's rainbow screen
The auto's solid push
The phone's link with distant home
And the medicines which guard my health.
I praise You in the smell of creosote after rain
In the aroma of a Sonoran enchilada
The scent of the lake on a hot summer day
Cinnamon buns baking on the stove
Evergreen needles at Christmas time
The rosemary bush at the dawn of spring
Channel number 5 on an opera night
Hot chocolate frothing in a mug
I praise You in all my loves.
Amen.

February 14, 1992 — Tucson

My Love,

Valentine's day! A feast of lovers! Why, I wonder this morning, has the church been so skeptical of romantic love and
continues to be even to this day? One part of the church, I should
say, because the other part is responsible for this delightful (and
now, in a nice twist, highly commercial) festival. Well, the tendency is against that old cynical prudery, but the latter has hung
on for a long time and won't give up easily. It is strange that
every time at a wedding I suggest that human passion is a sacrament, people are surprised (and mostly pleased). Oh, yes, there is
a long way to go.

At the center of the experience of romantic love is the notion
that I need the beloved and the beloved needs me. That's fine
with human lovers but I run into a philosophical and psychological barrier when I try to apply it to my relationship with You (to
say nothing of the resistance I encounter when I try to preach it).

As I have said repeatedly, You so describe Yourself in the
Scriptures. Moreover, I make the qualification that when one
talks about You one is always using metaphors — You are *like*
the romantic lover who needs the beloved. You are also utterly
different, but the metaphor tells me something about You.

I think of one of the friends I love who was on the phone last
night utterly distraught about problems that are both real and not
real. Are You that distraught? About me? Can I console You the
way I console?

I have to say that there was something in that conversation
which is a metaphor for my relationship with You and Your relationship with me. Console God? It almost sounds blasphemous,
but there is an important component of truth in it that I must
learn and so must everyone else. Console You over the sufferings
of others (the boy who drowned in California yesterday)?

The answer has to be "yes" but there's a lot more reflection
required.

Anyway, happy Valentine's day!

February 18, 1992 — Tucson

My Love,

I finished this morning reading a long — and often impenetrable — poem about Your Son's good friend John the Evangelist (though I don't think they called him "Evangelist" in those days). The poem at least makes the point that Jesus cared deeply for John and that often this was too much for John to absorb. Also he was not able to escape from Your Son's love.

Naturally.

It's so hard to accept the fact that we are loved, isn't it? I'm sure that's not a problem with You. In this respect, human behavior is *not* a metaphor for You, is it? It has been hard for me during my life to appreciate, much less cope with or respond to, the love people feel for me.

I would not have made so many mistakes, particularly with my ill-fated parish community, if I had been aware of the intensity of their affection (and in that case their ambivalence) for me. I simply did not, could not believe that I stirred up such strong (and often destructive) emotions. Even today I am a little surprised at how many people actually like me. There are things to be done, projects to be finished, there is no time to consider affection much less to respond to it.

Part of it perhaps was my seminary training in which we were warned against human affection (even for our families!) as though human love were not sacramental. They were worried, of course, about sexual love, as though there were any love which did not have a sexual component in it. They wanted to prevent us from falling in love with and then sinning with women. Perhaps the latter was a legitimate goal, but they drove men to women (as we found when so many left the priesthood after the Council) by denying them the possibility of all human affection.

I'm no longer worried about that fear, at least not compulsively worried about it, and I'm sure the seminary only reenforced a dimension of my personality which made it difficult for me to attend to human love.

I think, finally after a lifetime, I'm beginning to understand that many people love me, that indeed I am extremely fortunate in the multiplicity of loves in my life. Still I don't pay enough at-

tention to those loves (beyond the responsibilities) or enjoy them
enough.

And even less to Your love for me, which I do believe and
do profess but to which I pay so little heed in the course of an
ordinary day. And even worse on a day like yesterday. For which
I am sorry.

I'll be back to that love tomorrow. Help me to live it a little
better today.

February 19, 1992 — Tucson

My Love,

I finished reading Harold Bloom's *The Book of J* yesterday. It's
an odd book, anti-Catholic and professedly agnostic, but brilliant. It's about You and about the first real record we have of
what You're like, the "J" fragment of the Hebrew Bible. The book
is very controversial and doubtless exaggerated and wrong in
many respects. Yet I think in one fundamental sense he's right.

Is the author of that Scripture, whom he calls "J," really a
woman? The best argument is that the author presents stronger
and more attractive women then men. But so do I in my novels,
and many other male novelists and filmmakers as well. Hence a
dubious argument to say the least. The thesis is that the author,
on whose work all subsequent Jewish and Christian traditions
depend for their primal vision of You, is recording in literary
form her interpretation of the religious experience of her tradition and people. We get at ancient Jewish religion through the
filter of "J." Fair enough. Bloom also says the author is neither religious nor God-obsessed but is rather ironic, which also may be
fair enough, though I think there's some projection there.

But the core of the argument is that You are experienced as
pure exuberant vitality and that the "Promise" is a promise of
life, more life, superabundant life. I think this insight is probably
correct — our religion is based on a vision of You as exuberant
energy. What else could You possibly be? Somehow that vision
coheres with what contemporary science has to say and to my
own notion of You as a "teenage" God. Probably not surprisingly
since I am influenced by "J" as much as by anyone else. It is not

sexual energy, says Bloom, but about that one may be skeptical. I've often wondered why You present Yourself as Love, when love — as the old Audrey Hepburn / Albert Finney film I saw last night — is such a raw, messy, primal, irrational thing. I have thought often You do so because the vitality and drive of love is a good metaphor, indeed the best, for Yourself.

Bloom's interpretation of J seems to fit that too, even if he doesn't perceive it.

He sees the rest of the tradition as essentially an attempt to tame You, to "clean up" Your image. Surely there is something odd and even capricious about Your behavior in the J fragment, but not so odd if the metaphor is really one of headlong vitality. Perhaps the metaphor needed some correction, though, as Bloom notes, Your "character" seems to grow in the story as You become more "Self-reflective."

Certainly much of religion, including the terrible people in the Vatican today, has been an attempt to tone down Your vitality, to pretty up the fury of Your love. I have the impression that You might not like that.

Exuberant vitality is not easy to cope with, according to Bloom. Much of the tragedy of the lives of the characters in the story is the result of their being overwhelmed by that vitality, especially those "theomorphic" characters who are especially likely to represent You like Tamar and Zipporah and Jacob. Tragedy is rooted in the vitality of being, an interesting idea.

February 22, 1992 — Tucson

My Love,

The poem I read this morning from the book of spiritual poems is from the Upanishads. It compares lovers at the height of sexual ecstasy with the person who is in union with God. The former are aware at their time of union of nothing else. So with the latter. To be united with God (Self they call You) is to eliminate all other problems or worries from Your consciousness.

I can't disagree with the metaphor or the truth contained in it. However, it reveals how impoverished my own spiritual life is. I am so preoccupied by so many different problems and projects that I have little time for You and almost no peace. And this is after a lifetime of trying. I'm worried now about my work. And I worry about the pedophile crisis in Chicago. Either the cardinal and the church make a gigantic leap forward away from the problem or there will be terrible trouble. I am in the odd position of hoping for a little more trouble to avoid a lot more trouble. But these two problems, almost compulsively preoccupying these last few days, have destroyed my peace and interfered with my prayer.

I can't let go of them; they're real problems. Neither would the two lovers in the poem let go of similar problems. My challenge — a lifelong one — has been to honor my obligations and commitments and still have time for You. I've improved a little bit but not much as these past two days have demonstrated. It's so difficult to balance the two worlds, so very difficult.

Next week I will add to my responsibilities a guest. I'm delighted always by guests, but I must juggle more things when I have a guest. I'm not able to let go of the other responsibilities and my relationships with You suffer.

I know that the guest is You and that in welcoming the guest I welcome You. So if I'm not at this screen every morning bright and early, You understand.

My impatience is with myself; it is not with You or Your love. I know You love me the way I am. I just wish I was a little better, a little closer to You.

February 23, 1992 — Tucson

My Love,

The translation of the psalm I read for this morning says in effect that happy are those who know how to leave things the way they are. I'm not sure that's what the psalmist had in mind, to tell the truth. And it is hardly compatible with the image of You as pure vitality and energy, life abundant and superabundant. There is a kernel of important wisdom in that meaning however. There are some things that one can change. But no one can change everything. I certainly overcommit myself to changing things. For example this crusade on which I have embarked against pedophile priests. It's a valid crusade and at least one priest has to stand up against the problem. That part is all right, but now it's become a personal battle as was the Cody battle. I don't say that I should do anything less than I have done, but I do say that my assumption of responsibility and, to be more precise, my worry about it as a personal responsibility is excessive.

Or is it?

My friend the priest psychologist says I'm obsessed about it because I was molested by my father. That is bullshit. You should excuse the expression but You know I'm not obsessed, and I ought not to let the success or failure of the crusade — it all hangs in the balance now — so heavily influence my psychological well-being.

"Teach me to care and not to care."

I'm going to have a guest this week, one that will add to the fun of life. Help me not let work responsibilities and the crusade interfere with the fun. Only with Your help and Your love can I carry it off.

I love You.

February 24, 1992 — Tucson

My Love,

The *New York Times* carried Peter Steinfels's story on pedophilia in Chicago today, a major victory, because the cardinal publicly accepts lay review boards and says he will not reassign such men. It has been a long fight for him and a somewhat shorter one for me. Peter has me "prodding" the cardinal, a verb that I'm not comfortable with. It's a major step towards the solution to the problem. I'm grateful to You for Your grace in this effort. We don't have perfect success yet, but today's article means that we have basically won. I hope it all works out soon. It would be good to have it off my mind.

Stay with me please through the week.

I love You.

February 27, 1992 — Tucson

My Love,

The psalm I read in a new translation this morning celebrates You because of the beauty and order in creation, a celebration that is appropriate in this lovely desert spring. I found myself reflecting once again on how much we lost because of the textbook arguments about Your existence. Order and beauty prove that You are only to those who already believe it. Once we reduce order and beauty to an argument, we are open to the attacks of "science," which "explains" order and beauty by explaining them away.

This "science" is misguided because our knowledge of the mechanisms of order and beauty ought not to make them any less wonderful. Nor should such knowledge be taken to settle the question of Order and Beauty, which continues to exist.

I have felt for many years that order and beauty of the sort that are celebrated in the psalms are much more appropriate for describing *what* You're like than *whether* You are. That You are is suggested by the fact that anything is. What You are is a much more important question. You are like the loveliness of this spring morning, a morning which I am likely to defile before too many minutes are over in a mad rush to catch up with my schedule. At least, I beg You, let me savor it for a few moments.

February 28, 1992 — Tucson

My Love,

Simplicity, compassion, patience — those are the virtues urged on me by my readings about the Tao this morning. I measure in pretty well on compassion and badly, I fear, on the other two. I am not a simple person. I'm not sure I was designed to be a simple person, and I know I have not lived a simple life. I am a complicated and often contradictory character, a local by commitment and choice, a wandering cosmopolitan by circumstance. I believe in neighborhoods; I have none. I believe in place, and I have no single place. Moreover, now that I have some reasons to develop a sense of locale and a couple of places to belong to, I have spread myself out so thin that I'm unable to do so.

I have a number of different critical professions, priest above all else, but writer, storyteller, sociologist, journalist, and more recently crusader.

Given my range of interests I probably could be a lot more if there were enough hours in the day — and as I demonstrated this week when I had a guest, there are not enough hours in the day when even one additional opportunity is added. I rush, rush, rush. Not exactly simple, is it?

I don't know what to do. I've got to ponder this business of simplicity a little more. My world is too complicated by half, but I don't know how to get out of it or even whether You would really want me to.

Help, please. I love You.

February 29, 1992 — Tucson

My Love,

I continue to reflect on simplicity on this rainy day during which I have struggled with computer systems, article revisions, phone calls, and such like, and worry about the pedophile situation and the church and anything else that crosses my mind today.

In the midst of all this complexity, is it possible to find simplicity, a simplicity underlying complexity? I hope it is, but I haven't found the way to do it yet. I really must ponder this; it's an important issue for the rest of my life. Maybe "cutting back" is not the right perspective. Maybe the change needs to be more internal than external. Or maybe when it's internal the external will become more obvious.

On another subject I had an angry dream about my days at Christ the King the other night, forcing me once again to consider whether I have really forgiven my pastor from that era. I was never reconciled with him — as I was with the cardinal. But he was unlike the cardinal in that he oppressed me and others intolerably. Can I ever forget those incidents and the bizarre social controls he exercised?

I wish we had been reconciled before his death. I wish I had even thought of it. Maybe later on. In Your world to come.

I love You.

March 1992

March 1, 1992 — Tucson

My Love,

I quote from Stephen Mitchell's anthology of religious poetry a segment of the Bhagavad Gita: "I am always with all beings / I abandon no one. And / However great your inner darkness / You are never separate from me. / Let your thoughts flow past you, calmly; / Keep me with your life, because I / *am* you, more than you yourself are."

That's pretty good, isn't it? And I really believe it. In my head. In the worrying parts of my soul I don't act like it very much, do I? You are more me than I myself am!

What an exciting notion. You suffer with me, as I told the *Tribune* reporter who interviewed me about evil yesterday. You will take care of me in the long run. You know what demons beset me, and You will struggle with me against them.

You are more me than I am! How wonderful!

I have not lived that way. Not often. I have struggled against life with determination and talent and that's all right, so long as I realize You struggle with me and will take care of me in my ultimate defeats, defeats which are as certain as death.

If I believe even a little bit that You are more me than I am, my life would indeed be simpler, not in its schedule but in my reaction to the schedule, not in its troubles but in my response to its troubles, not in its responsibilities but in my grace in the face of the responsibilities.

There is still a lot to do, as You surely know. Maybe I can be a little more simple in the way I do it.

March 2, 1992 — Tucson

My Love,

In the Eastern religious segments I am reading these days, there is great wisdom, but I wonder if I should buy it without notable modifications. Thus when one writer says there is no today or yesterday or tomorrow but all is one, he speaks an important truth — life is rapidly passing and even something of an illusion. But he also implies what I take to be an untruth. For today is not yesterday and it is not tomorrow. Teach us to care and not to care, as T. S. Eliot said in what has now become a cliché but is not less true than when he wrote it. I have no trouble caring, but not caring? Ah, that's another matter. You surely want me to care. Help me to learn in the few years of life left to me how also not to care.

March 6, 1992 — Tucson

My Love,

The Bible says that "in You we live and move and have our being." St. Mechtild of Magdeburg (whose name has always delighted me) says that we move in You like the bird in the air, the fish in the water. What a lovely comparison! Men and women of deep faith and mystical insight are always trying to say something like that and are, I think, never quite satisfied with their metaphors. They have penetrated into the Great Secret of the universe, one that gives life meaning and purpose and joy, and they try desperately to share it with the rest of us who are caught up in the cares and responsibilities and anxieties of life. Moreover we don't doubt the truth of what they say; on the contrary, at least in my case, I absolutely believe it. But the demands are still there. Like the bird I fly through the air unaware that Love is sustaining and protecting me. Like the fish I swim through the sea not realizing how You envelop and absorb me. Like the lover who takes his love for granted I am immersed in Love and hardly recognize it.

In rereading my own journal for the day I encounter again my awareness of wonder, frail and illusive as that awareness is, and wonder why I don't wonder. The answer is that I am too busy, rushing around about minor things, and I don't wonder enough at the medical school building, for example, glowing as if it had been whitewashed in the sun breaking through the rain clouds — You washing the world clean and renewing it.

I believe in wonder and surprise. I believe You renew everything. I believe that I am bathed in Your love. Help me during the fundamentally unpleasant day ahead of me to me a bit more aware of Your love.

I don't want to go back to Chicago and yet I do want to go home. Maybe I should view the whole Arizona interlude as a wonder experience.

I am deeply grateful for it. Help me to go home happy and relaxed.

I love You.

March 9, 1992 — Tucson

Another pedophile case in Chicago and another explosion. When will they ever learn!

I reread in my own journal (of which I've probably read enough to know about the person who wrote it — strange man) an entry quoting an Irish writer about how as Creator You are superior to us but as Lover You are almost inferior — a powerful image if there ever was one, and one which I can't quite cope with although I believe it's true and indeed celebrate it in my novels.

I'll have to try to do it again in the next novel, which is taking a vague shape in my head.

That You depend on me as a lover is a metaphor which could transform my life if I really believed it and also slowed down my life. Or would it? How much of my life (a half dozen phone calls already, looking like it's going to be one of those days) is a response to You as You choose to manifest Yourself in the brothers and sisters. I guess I have to work harder at seeing You in them.

However, one does not work at love, not, I suspect, even with an invisible Lover.

However, are not all lovers to some extent invisible?

Anyway, I'm eager to get home, though it looks like it's going to be hellish for the first couple of days.

March 11, 1992 — Tucson

My Love,

A very nice quote from Angelus Silesius this morning: "God whose love and joy / are everywhere / can't come to visit you / unless you aren't there."

Like the little man who wasn't there and still isn't there today?

Well, no. I'm joking. But the idea is great, especially if one puts an emphasis on the *You*. The ego has to retreat for You to come. However, it can't disappear or the love affair becomes impossible. One can have a love affair only if there are two persons, two "thous" present. Still the point is well taken: No love affair can long subsist if one partner is totally preoccupied with the self and has little concern for the other-as-person. I'm too much here for there to be room for You to visit.

I'm still very much in the way, very much concerned about all my worries, still leaving so little room for You to invade my life.

I'm sorry. Help me to do better.

I also want to thank You again for this Tucson interlude, which means so much to my life and health even if the demands here are as bad as they are in Chicago. I wish I were going home relaxed and refreshed, but at least I'm not going home exhausted as was true in days gone by. Thanks very much for this part of my life.

March 12, 1992 — Somewhere over Texas

My Love,

I'm in the plane flying home to Chicago. As I look at the Tucson interlude, I note that I finished the assignments that I gave myself before I left Chicago. I revised two books and learned the Windows system. I'm afraid I did not relax much as I had planned to do, though there were lots of times of afternoon warmth outside, which were certainly rejuvenating. My prayer didn't get any better, but it didn't get any worse, and at least I learned a few things about myself and about You.

But You continue to be a mystery to me, all too often a distant mystery, a lover I want to know better but for whom I just don't seem to have enough time. I do indeed write these reflections every day, but they are no substitute for the silent contemplation which I would like to do but of which my racing, distracted imagination with its permeable boundaries does not seem capable.

I hope in this quarter — mid-March to mid-June if You will — to try some contemplation again and to try to listen to You throughout the day, a task which I blew completely during my harried time in Tucson. I will also do my article about religion and the Brits and try to write another novel. I really should be doing a bit of fiction all the time, if I can without racing through a story for closure. How else does one improve? In the sociology I'll be playing with the new SPSS (computer statistics program) so I can learn that better. A not unreasonable three months. Only four trips, Tampa, Toledo, New Orleans, and Spartanburg, with perhaps a side trip to New York if there seems any purpose in it.

Thank You for my good health and good fortune. I love You very much.

March 15, 1992 — Chicago

The St. Patrick's Day Mass was lovely. Enough to bring a tear or two to my eye as I thought of all those who came before me and suffered so that I might be able to have the life I have, a life about which I might complain less if I stopped to think about the men and women on whose shoulders I stand.

Death has claimed them all as it will some day in the not too distant future claim me. I hope I can say that I love You as much as they did, given the advantages I have enjoyed in my life. I'm not sure that's true however.

The pedophile mess in Chicago is even worse than I thought it might be. Apparently only an explosion will cure it, if that.

I hope I can contemplate Your love more this week and all the weeks to come back home here in Chicago.

And, I hasten to add, it's wonderful to be home again. Thank You for this gorgeous city and all the friends I have here.

March 16, 1992 — Chicago

My Love,

I'm surrounded by a lot of beauty today. It's cold out but the sun shines and the city is spectacularly lovely. Also last night I watched the end of *Fantasia* and a tape about Chicago skyscrapers. The former was cute and clever, nothing much more, but not all that bad for its age, and the latter did what art is supposed to do — it made me see things for the first time. I must visit the lobbies of the five buildings the next time I'm in the Loop. I never really noticed them before — or the other beautiful lobbies all scattered throughout this fantastic city.

And I heard the first act of Ed McKenna's new opera. His score is superb, and my libretto makes it move swiftly. Whether it is good enough to make it into the repertory of the Lyric or not remains to be seen, but it certainly is good. Again so much beauty.

So many reflections of You and Your goodness.

And the usual stupidities and deaths in the news this morning. Again the terrible dilemma of good and evil in the world of You, and of bad things. I believe in You but I'm horrified by the bad things, particularly just now by the bad things priests are doing to children. I'm heavily involved now, despite myself, in a campaign to make it stop. Jousting with windmills again, though in this case the windmills deserve to be torn down. Please help the cardinal to make the right decisions. He doesn't have much time left.

I love You. Thank You for all the beauty.

March 17, 1992 — Chicago

My Love,

St. Patrick's day and election day. I'm displeased with both, the election because there is so much nonsense in American elections and such unspeakable candidates. One votes against people instead of for them, to settle scores rather than to change the country. Just now it doesn't look like the country will be changed.

And, as You well know, no one in this city is more Irish than I am. I've written books, columns, articles, novels celebrating the Irish. The American Irish are the matrix out of which my imagination works.

Yet St. Patrick's day bores me. Too much of it is dumb, insensitive, arrogant, as though we are trying to live up to the stereotypes others have created for us.

I hope as my Lover You understand this mood better than I do.

March 18, 1992 — Chicago

My Love,

As You may remember (of course You do, but I'm being polite!) I've had a hard time with the New Testament lately because the biblical criticism which I've read through the years, however brilliant it may be, has reduced the story to its component parts. Which is more historical, the Sermon on the Mount of Matthew or the Sermon on the Plain of Luke? What can we know about the historical Jesus? These are not unimportant issues, particularly for scholars and apologists. Clearly with men like Dom Crosson flitting around saying that Jesus was nothing more than an ingenious peasant, those questions have to be asked. Unfortunately, they are not the questions most people ask and the answers to them are not responsive to most people's needs, including my own. So the new "literary" approach to the Scripture ought to be a big help. The problem with it is that good literary criticism requires a different kind of talent than exegetical scholarship. The man who searches out the story must have almost the same perspective as a storyteller. At least he must respect the storyteller

It looks like I've found a good book (courtesy of Jack Shea) or rather two good books, Tannehill's two-volume *The Narrative Unity of Luke-Acts*. I started to read it this morning and it looks like it will be my spiritual reading for a long time to come. Thank You for bringing it to my attention and help me to learn more about You and Your love from it.

March 21, 1992 — Chicago

My Love,

The first day of spring, but still winter in Chicago. We seem to have had winter in the autumn and the spring this year. The papers are calling it "Indian Winter." Paul Tsongas withdrew from the presidential race, leaving it all to Clinton, another disaster for the country, one that it enhances my ongoing depression.

Well, anyway. My reading of Tannehill on St. Luke this morning was profitable, though hardly for lifting my spirits. He points out the bittersweet nature of the canticles in the infancy narrative. They are exuberant outbursts of joy, the Magnificat especially strong in its celebration of Your bursting into history. But the readers of the gospel will know that the joy was inappropriate or at least premature. For the response to Your good news revealed in Jesus notably impaired its success. Jesus was rejected, indeed by his own people but in fact in great part by everyone, including those who claim to be following him, myself included.

As the late Gus Weigel (be good to him, please) once remarked, "All human efforts, given time, go badly."

The rejection of the good news, so vigorously celebrated in the infancy stories, the turning of our backs on Your intervention in our history in and through Jesus, is both tragic and mysterious. And temporary. You will win out in the long run. Just now it looks very long indeed.

As I try to type out these reflections, the phone rings and I hear more about the pedophile suits.

Very, very long.

Help me, however, to understand that the joy of the infancy canticles is ultimate.

March 22, 1992 — Chicago

My Love,

St. Luke, I learn today (or perhaps relearn), was acutely aware of the growth of the self-consciousness of Jesus, a position which would offend not only fundamentalists but also a good many Catholic conservatives who would want him to have known in the crib that he was the second person of Your Trinity. Not only was the incident in the temple an indication of growth in age and wisdom and grace, but also the events at the Jordan and in the desert which lead up to his announcement of his mission at the synagogue in Nazareth, a mission which would become ever more clearly defined as his life went on.

Your Son, in other words, was always open to the promptings of the Spirit and often found it a struggle to comprehend those promptings and had to contend with temptations to ignore them.

The point for me this morning is not, however, the theology of the Incarnation or a rediscovery of the humanity of Jesus; rather for me the insight and the challenge is the need to be open. As I think about our up-coming fiftieth grammar school reunion, I marvel at how different I am from what anyone would have expected then, myself included.

I don't claim that I have always been responsive to Your Spirit (witness the mess I made of my relationship with the cardinal). I have been responsive enough, however, to trod a path which in prospect would have seemed most unlikely and now in retrospect seems quite incredible. I am grateful for the overwhelming grace with which You seduced me down this path.

Where does the path lead to next, that is the issue on this second day of spring with eight inches of snow on the ground. I don't know. I have followed the Spirit without much reflection down through the decades of my life. I must continue to do so, trying to be responsive to what happens. The temptation for me is not to make a wrong decision; it is rather to think that the path is near an end and to strive for a bit more rationality and order.

"Relax and enjoy the fruits of your work," one of my acquaintances advised me when she was inveighing against my novels. That's the temptation. It may be a little bit stronger now than it used to be. Help me to resist it.

March 23, 1992 — Chicago

My Love,

In St. Luke I learn the emphasis is on the teaching and healing of Jesus, and in the former on his evangelizing (verb used more than the noun). Jesus went around preaching good news! And no one believed him. How totally weird. Do we believe him now? Not really. I mean, we profess to believe him but we don't act or live like we do and we reduce the good news to burdens and responsibilities and rules. Even "evangelization" as a catchword and a cliché has been stripped of its meaning. It's another burden imposed by enthusiasts who really wouldn't inspire anyone to believe in good news.

Contrasting the pedophile mess with Jesus going around preaching good news is ironic indeed. We are a very imperfect species, are we not?

I do my best to preach good news both in my stories at Mass and in my fiction. Help me always by word and deed, by manner and visage, by life and work to reflect to some small extent the joy which good news ought to bring.

And please help us through this terrible pedophile crisis.

March 25, 1992 — Chicago

My Love,

I've taken time off from reading about St. Luke to go through Jack Shea's new book on beholding Christmas all year round (*Starlight*) — a masterpiece written in terrible health. I hope he comes back from Mayo's with some kind of treatment for his severe back pain.

There is in the book a marvelous quote from one of Chesterton's early poems about good news, which is appropriate for my current set of reflections with You.

> Good News: But if you ask me what it is, I know not;
> It is a track of feet in the snow,
> It is a lantern showing a path;
> It is a door set open

That seems to say it perfectly. No, not so much to say it, because it can't be said, but to image it. The good news which Jesus preached is a track of feet, a path illumined by a lantern, an open door — a direction, an invitation, a welcome, a hint of a beloved who is waiting.

All Jesus did was to confirm that image, to say in effect, yes, there is an invitation, a beloved who is waiting. That for which we hope in the deepest moments of human longing really does exist; that is the good news. To say "all" of what Jesus did, however, is not to make it minor or unimportant. There is nothing more important than to confirm that people's brightest dreams can and do come true.

Yet people didn't want to hear that. They still don't. Some reject it explicitly; others, while proclaiming its truth, don't want to live with the consequences. I'm in the latter category, but at least I know that the path is there, the light is shining, and the door is open.

I love You.

March 26, 1992 — Chicago

My Love,

Christmas, Jack says in his powerful book, is reality. All the rest of the year is illusion. At Christmas we celebrate the union between spirit and flesh which we humans are and through which You reveal Yourself. We also celebrate Mary's "Yes," the anniversary date of which was yesterday. As for myself I can only agree with the illusion of all else besides Christmas and the necessity of a constant and ongoing "yes."

But I'm so tired. And so deeply involved in so many things. And feel spread out so thin. And find it so hard to get going in the morning. Or stay awake after supper at night. Or to be cheery on the phone when I'm constantly interrupted (starting at 8:00 A.M. yesterday). Minor annoyances indeed. But given the frailty of the human condition minor distractions and troubles which make it almost impossible to look up and see the stars, the stars of Christmas or of any other time.

Last night when I was about to collapse into bed I looked out the window and saw the wondrous sight of the city stretched out beneath me. How beautiful it was. How much it told me about You. But I was too worn out to be able to pay any attention to it. I admired briefly and then went to bed. I'm sorry.

I'm sorry I was so grumpy in late afternoon yesterday, but I could hardly keep my eyes open. Christmas all year round, indeed. But I'm pretty worn out at Christmas too.

I realize that I'm writing about the basic limitations of being human and that You understand and love me just the same. I hope You continue to love me, as of course You will. And if You could give me a little more energy, I'd be very grateful indeed.

March 27, 1992 — Chicago

My Love,

Jack is back with no diagnosis and no cure but feeling somewhat better. I hope You can take care of him, because we all need his wit and his wisdom desperately.

In the second-to-the-last chapter of his book this morning he talks about Christmas and death, the phenomenon of recalling our dead friends and family at Christmas and often becoming depressed and melancholy about them. He suggests that it is not inappropriate, nor is it inappropriate to think of Good Friday on Christmas because the Crucifixion is as much part of the Incarnation of You in the flesh of Jesus as is his conception and birth. You took on human flesh in the person of Jesus to reveal concretely and visually the extent and the power of Your love for us. You "emptied" Yourself in love, even to the death of the cross, so we would know that the love which the prophets understood was at least as powerful as the prophets thought and at least as intimate.

Why don't we preach that central truth more? Why don't we

practice it more? Why are we so tied up in rules and institutional questions? Again it is a case, I suppose, of the good news being too good to be true. We don't want to preach "too much" love for fear that it will encourage the faithful to sin if they know that they are loved that way. We won't be able to keep them in line. Or we might let up on ourselves if we realized how loving God is. The dead are already fully aware of that love and are, Jack suggests, perhaps even closer to us now than they were when they were alive because God is so intimate with us.

The purpose of the Incarnation was to reveal love, love like that of the father of the prodigal son, a love which would follow along with its beloved even to the death of the cross.

Hard to comprehend? You bet. But the point is not to comprehend it but to believe it and live it — and not reduce it to a cliché. That's not part of my consciousness yet, save on rare occasions, but it should be and I want it to be and I beg You to help me to be more conscious of it than I am, especially as I race through life trying to juggle so many projects and responsibilities.

I am loved extravagantly, indeed with the kind of emptying of Self which is beyond the most passionate of human loves.

To say to You that I love You in return seems a weak and sorry response, but it is all of which I am capable and I know that it's all You want. Help me to do it more often and more consciously and more fully

March 28, 1992 — Chicago

My Love,

The long poem which ends Jack's book (and which I've read before and reflected on before) ends with the listener going into the cave at Bethlehem and discovering that s/he is the "beloved child."

Like a lot of Jack's other metaphors this one is so shocking that many readers will think it is merely a pious exaggeration instead of a "true" story. Hence they'll miss the point — and the more conservative will scream "heresy." But that each of us is a "beloved child," a continuation of the Incarnation, and that You disclose Yourself in each of us as well as in Jesus are truths which cannot be denied, even if they are so often ignored.

There are many ways to go from that insight — greater value of the self, deeper realization of how much You love each of us, a more powerful awareness of our revelatory vocation, a richer sense of unity between the human and the divine, between humanity and divinity, between You and us.

It is easy to conclude that one is unimportant in the scheme of things. We live for a few years and then disappear from the scene. Most of what we dream of doesn't come true, we experience more failures than successes, our bodies break down, our loves often do not work out, we think we become wise and in fact only become cynical. We are soon completely forgotten. Moreover we can be snuffed out of existence by a drunken driver, a drug-crazed mugger, a faulty panel in a plane, random bad luck. An accidental being brought accidently to life and dying, in one form or another, an accidental death.

Yet, we are also God's beloved child — *Your* beloved child. Of infinite worth and appeal like every child is to its parents (as the kids were at the home I visited last night). We do not appreciate ourselves enough, we do not love ourselves enough, we do not luxuriate in our own dignity and importance enough, we do not face the darkness ahead with confidence enough. We do not see the lantern and the open door clearly enough.

I do not understand it at all. I don't see why You love us so much, but love is never understandable. You do love us, as the father of the prodigal son loved both his sons, and that must mean that we are far more appealing than we can possibly imagine. I am far more appealing to You than I can possibly imagine.

The Beloved Child!

March 29, 1992 — Chicago

My Love,

The second theme of the "beloved child" metaphor is the depth and power of Your love for us, one that I've wrestled with for years and have never been able to make much of — insofar as comprehending it and transforming my life with it. The "beloved child" metaphor merely is another way of exploring the theme of Incarnation. When Your Son became human, *all of us* were revealed as "beloved children." Not only was he born in Bethlehem, so were we, so was the whole of humanity. This was of course very good news indeed. Our birth was in fact a rebirth as well as a birth, a theme which St. Luke constantly repeats in his emphasis on the forgiveness of sinners. Of course one forgives beloved children.

How far have we come from that revelation. We continue to be obsessed by sin and punishment, by power and prestige as though the Incarnation and the forgiveness inherent in it never happened.

Yet how welcome that message of forgiveness is when it is preached. It is surely the most powerful theme in my novels and gains the most enthusiastic reactions.

Oh, yes, You love us beyond any limit that we can possibly imagine. Why You do so is not evident and cannot be explained, but that does not matter. You *do* love us and that is enough.

If only we could believe it and live that way.

What dull, rigid creatures we are! But apparently not the way You see us. You forgive even our reluctance to believe that we are forgiven. How much like the father of the prodigal son.

Help me to understand and comprehend and live by this truth.

March 30, 1992 — Chicago

My Love,

Today I'm off to St. Petersburg, Florida, for a panel with the Rabbi. But first I want to reflect on the "beloved child" metaphor as it suggests the revelatory role of each one of us. You incarnate Yourself especially in Jesus, but also in all of us who share humanity with him. Others are to see You in us. I confess I don't feel much like a sacrament, though I know I've learned that I am for many people, especially through the novels and the columns. Whether my goodness and joy, my openness and happiness, have also been sacramental is another question. I suppose the answer is sometimes yes, sometimes no. I try, often not hard enough. And I'm so often tired and unresponsive.

These past weeks, since I've come back to Chicago from Tucson, I seem to have been especially sluggish, tied down by my weary, aging body. And I haven't been in the classroom yet. There is not much savor in my life right now; the salt has lost its savor, or so it seems. To be revelatory means to be the salt of the earth and the light of the world. Now I feel I'm just going through the motions.

Not enough vitality or energy to be a good sacrament, I'm afraid. Just running on empty.

I must keep working while there is still some light.

I love You.

April 1992

April 2, 1992 — Chicago

My Love,

On the plane back from Tampa yesterday I read most of Paul Davis's book *The Mind of God,* an interesting argument for Your existence based on the laws of nature. The laws, he said, didn't have to exist; neither did the initial conditions; neither did our ability to recognize these laws through math; nor finally did the universe itself have to exist. Thus You do. Not a bad reformulation of the old argument from design, nothing more than a probabilistic argument but powerful nonetheless. One point is that the cosmos in which we live may well be designed to produce the maximum amount of variety consistent with some kind of organized structure. That I like especially because of my metaphor about You as a teenage woman! But You *should* produce a variegated universe. Why not? It gives a powerful image of Your exuberance, another teenage characteristic, if I may say so.

That thought brings me to the fourth aspect of the beloved child metaphor — the unity between humanity and divinity, an always existing unity which was redisclosed, reenforced, and presented as an even deeper unity in the Incarnation of Jesus. I suppose if I said this in public I'd have to make the usual pro forma rejection of pantheism, which the heresy hunters always shout. Clearly You and we are not the same but we are also united in the act of creative love. I'm not my characters in the novels, but they exist in my mind too, another metaphor which

is appropriate. The Incarnation in Jesus is categorically different from the incarnation in us, but they are not totally dissimilar
either because You disclose Yourself in us too.

Others know You through me! What a terrifying thought,
especially when I'm tired and irritable and discouraged. Yet I believe it and want to act as if I believe it. Help me today and in
days and weeks to come to understand this truth: You live in me,
not only as a lover but, because as a lover, also as self-revealer.

April 3, 1992 — Chicago

My Love,

I forgot how much I like teaching! The class was great fun
yesterday — good, intelligent, responsive students and only
about twenty so I can get to know their names and their background. Thanks again for the opportunity. I'd like to do more of
it, but there are so many things I like to do.

The new pedophile suit broke yesterday with all the bad publicity for the church. Predictably it reacted with references to
police reports. No one will believe them, I'm afraid, except the
most devout Catholic laity who want to believe regardless.

I don't know where it will all end. But it got worse yesterday.
The church is paying, in spades, for its past sins.

I regret ever having become involved.

The church's lawyers are going after the _____ this afternoon. In addition to being vicious this will make the settlement
of that suit almost impossible. Greek tragedy.

St. Luke's Gospel, with its neat reversal stories, emphasizes
Jesus' mission to the poor and the oppressed, the sick and the
disadvantaged. It has been used to justify liberation theology,
though the people who so use it are hardly oppressed themselves
and their "identification with the poor" is patronizing and phony
and the political system they wish to impose to help the poor is
tyrannical and, as we now know beyond any doubt, incompetent.

The pedophile victims and their families certainly belong in
the category of the oppressed; so do the blue collar workers who
suffer because of affirmative action; so do the union people at
Caterpillar and Hormel and other places who are being squeezed

out of their jobs; so do the white collar workers who are bounced without benefits from long-held jobs to make up for the mistakes of company executives (who collect big salaries). None of these people are politically correct; few worry about them because they are not black or gay or women. Surely many in the politically correct groups have also been victims, though membership in any group is not an automatic sign of oppression and victimization. I must not in my repugnance for political correctness deny past and present oppression of members of those groups.

But if one is against oppression one has to be against it no matter who the victim is. Selective outrage is hypocrisy.

So I will continue the pedophile fight regardless of outcome.

Help me to continue to do so.

April 4, 1992 — Chicago

My Love,

Paul Davies attempts to probe Your mind in his interesting book. In the passage I read yesterday, he outlines the intricate and yet simple cleverness with which You managed to produce carbon molecules; without them life would not be possible. Carbon, like so many other "coincidences," looks like a plot. And, as Chesterton argued years ago, if there's a plot one begins to suspect a plotter.

The evidence of a plot makes the rational design of the universe an extraordinarily plausible thesis. I think the God of "cosmic coincidences" fits the image You convey in the Bible pretty well, a (You should excuse the expression) show-off God, an involved God, a God who cares. It took a lot of care to develop all those ingenious coincidences, a lot of involvement, and, if I may say so, a lot of pure fun! I can imagine You chortling over how You bring the three helium molecules together at just the right time to produce carbon and murmuring, "That will show them!"

I've been more conscious of You the last couple of days, but my consciousness of You is still so weak, so tentative; I am still so much the neophyte after all these years of trying. Help me to continue to improve — while there's still time.

Daylight saving time begins tomorrow, a fresher sign of spring than the sun's crossing the equator. May spring bring new joy to my life!

April 6, 1992 — Chicago

My Love,

How I love this time of year, so filled with promise and possibility. Willingly, enthusiastically I give up the hour of sleep as we "spring forward." I celebrate the light and warmth and foretaste of Your summer. As You know I've learned this year to celebrate the sacramentality of the dark too. I like its privacy, its closeness, its mystery, its charm. But I'm still a sunlight, daytime, summer person. And daylight saving — along with a bright day such as this morning — brings me closer to summer, a season which like life is all too fleeting.

I finished Davies's book last night (during timeouts in the NCAA championships!). It's a strange book; he seems to hesitate at the edge of faith, accepting more or less the argument from design as suiting his metaphysical tastes, but still not sure about You and wondering whether mysticism might be the answer. But one need not be a mystic to see the kind of Thou who lurks behind what he calls a "designer universe." One need only to be a bit of poet and see the metaphors lying around all over the place.

Who You are and why You are and why You do what You do are mysteries which boggle the mind. But that You are and that in some special way You are Love is clear and true to me.

But how lucky I am to be born into a tradition which has given me the eyes of faith, which has spared me the necessity of postulating billions of other universes so this one could emerge by chance.

April 7, 1992 — Chicago

My Love,

I continue through the commentary on Jesus' mission to the oppressed and the excluded in St. Luke's Gospel. Clearly Your

Son was not into being politically correct. The Samaritans, the sinful woman, the publicans were all completely incorrect.

I love You.

April 8, 1992 — Chicago

My Love,

I was so drained at the end of the day that I had a hard time sleeping. I can imagine how tough it must be on the cardinal. The emerging story is at once exhilarating and exhausting, fascinating and depressing.

It is also so ugly. I'll be glad when it's all over. Please grant that something can be done to protect the children and the church and the cardinal.

It has not been a dull life, as You well know. I thank You for all the graces and blessings.

April 9, 1992 — Chicago

My Love,

I'm truly worn out. The pedophile thing weighs heavy upon my soul. The lawyers the church hired for the priest are out of control. They want a trial; they have nothing to lose. They will be paid, and even if they lose the case, they've had a good time. The church has a lot to lose, even if they win the suit and Joe may well be destroyed by it. I've done all I can, and it's not been enough, not in the absence of a smoking gun. I should stop worrying about it, because there's nothing left in a way of a contribution I can make. But I care about the children and their families. And I care about the church and I care about the cardinal. Well, I'm not You and I can't do Your work for You. But I do pray that You intervene and prevent the worst kind of disasters.

Take care of everyone who ought to be taken care of!

I love You. Help me out of this discouragement. Maybe a nap this afternoon would be in order.

April 11, 1992 — Chicago

My Love,

On this rainy morning I want to reflect a bit on what might be a dangerous propensity to take responsibility for things, particularly in the church but everywhere else too. Perhaps one of the things which went wrong in the parish group so many years ago was my assuming responsibility for their lives. I did not propose to take away their freedom, but I worried about them and kept after them, parent-like. Small wonder that they were able to find grounds for saying that I was trying to run their lives. Concern and manipulation are separated by thin boundaries.

Similarly in the [Cardinal] Cody fracas I assumed responsibility for saving the archdiocese from that madman. I didn't succeed and got myself burned in the process, which perhaps served me right — though the harm he was doing to the archdiocese and the church impelled me. In both the parish and the papal elections I became deeply involved in trying to save the church by my own unaided efforts. Now I'm taking a lot of responsibility for resolving the pedophile crisis.

Who do I think I am? You?

It's taken me a long time to learn this lesson and the lesson, like so many lessons, is ambiguous. The conclusion is not that I should be totally uninvolved, nor that I should completely let go of my responsibility. The conclusion is rather that I ought to be more cautious in my assumptions of responsibilities and in the extent of my involvements. I ought to play it cooler, not *totally* cool as the teens would say, but somewhat cool. I can't do everything and I shouldn't try.

Hence in the pedophile mess I must cool it — do what I can but also back off a bit (as I think I did last night) so that my involvement will not be counterproductive.

Above all I must watch this dangerous propensity to be responsible for everything — to the extent of overinvolvement and counterproduction — as well as destruction of peace of mind.

It's a delicate and subtle distinction, but mature people learn to make such distinctions, don't they?

Help me. I love You.

April 12, 1992 — Chicago

My Love,

I like the reference in the St. Luke commentary today that not only did Zaccheus seek Your Son but Your Son sought him. Jesus came to seek as well as to be sought. You sent him to seek us, an intermediary in Your love affair with Your people. What a clever idea! Congratulations! How far have we come from that beginning.

I continue to believe that I am supporting the oppressed in this pedophile business. If I am right, the church is doing terrible things to the people and to You and the message of Your Son. I think I have at least temporarily assumed the right posture: I've done all I can do and for the time being it's in the hands of others. I still hold the microphone and I can still speak out again if needs be. But for the moment (by which I mean the time between now and Easter) I back off and wait to see what happens.

I will bring the laptop to Grand Beach and will thus be able to continue my conversations and reflections with You. I hope I can rehabilitate myself for the difficult month and a half ahead before I settle in up there for the summer. I love You.

April 13, 1992 — Grand Beach

My Love,

It's nice to be up here! The sun's out and the village looks cheery despite the total absence of greenery. But it's cold, cold, cold. It doesn't matter though. I'm at Grand Beach and I'm taking time off and I'm going to pray with You through Holy Week. I love You. Help me to have a grace-full week.

April 14, 1992 — Grand Beach

My Love,

I watched *Silas Marner* on a BBC tape last night. Very well done. The film had the sentimentality of the story and its settings captured the harsh realism of life in England at that time. It set me thinking about all the suffering in the human condition. Indeed Silas manages to find happiness, though the poor squire does not, in a nice application of the pietism of the nineteenth century. Still the squire tried.

More to the point, of course, is that it does not always work out that way in real life. I think of the kids who have been pedophile victims in Northbrook and how their lives have been ruined before they start. I think of all the Jews murdered by Police Battalion 100 as described in the book reviewed in the papers yesterday. I think of the sufferings of some of my classmates. I think of the hypocrisy in the priesthood.

No, it doesn't work out. There is an incredible amount of suffering and misery and agony in the world. David Lodge's new novel, *Paradise News*, which I am reading now, reflects, as some of his best work does, the hopelessness of so many lives. Even if his character manages to escape at the end, not everyone does.

I suppose this is the time to say how lucky I am and how thankful I ought to be. Indeed I have been lucky and I am thankful, but that doesn't solve the problem, does it?

The problem is insoluble. This week is not about a solution as much as it is an assertion of Your solidarity with us in the suffering which is part of our condition, a solidarity even to the death of the cross, a solidarity rooted in love so powerful as to be beyond our imagination.

I'm obviously going to do a lot of thinking and praying up here, both because of what I'm reading and my mood and the time of the year. Finally it comes down to that solidarity of love, doesn't it? When people shout "Why?" — and not without reason much of the time — the only answer is that *"I love You,"* and implicit in that is a promise that somehow, someday it will be all right.

It's a lot to demand of Your children, isn't it?

You could reply that in Jesus You gave us the best hint we will ever have of how much You do love us. If we believe in Jesus, that is the answer, as obscure as it often seems.

I do believe it, but as I have often said to You, my belief affects my life only part of the time and even then only partially. It's so hard to have an invisible Lover even if that Lover sends spectacular messages. Help me to have deeper and more effective faith before this week is over.

April 16, 1992 — Grand Beach

My Love,

I had another disturbing call about the pedophile mess yesterday and have developed a tentative new strategy for dealing with it, though I am not confident that it will work, not at all; but the string must be played out, and then what happens will happen. The weather continues to be gray and depressing and promises to be that way till Easter. And the river is still flooding the city.

I continue to be impressed that this week is a manifestation of Love and that all other interpretations are either derivative or obfuscating. So much of the old Holy Week piety emphasized the horror of Your Son's suffering and our responsibility and guilt for those sufferings. The piety was well intentioned, or at least relatively so (it was a way to keep people in line, I suppose). But the truth is that the death and resurrection of Jesus are a revelation of what You are like — not an accountant demanding atonement for sin, but a lover manifesting passion for us. I think I have discovered this for the first time, not because of anything I've read but because of my own reflections. Everything is designed to reveal You to us, especially the coming of Jesus. You wanted to join Your beloved creatures even to the abyss of death and thus give meaning to our lives and our deaths.

So this week is a week of rejoicing and happiness, not only on Sunday but all week long. I hope that this truly good news can pervade my life during the rest of the week.

Help me to have a good Holy Week. I love You.

April 18, 1992 — Chicago

My Love,

Holy Saturday, and Lent is almost over. Since I've been fasting this week, it's nice to know that Lent is almost at an end. I think one could keep Lent pretty easily if one stayed within the framework of the church institution, that is, lived in a rectory in a parish and ate most of one's meals in the rectory and did most of one's activity in the parish. But the life I lead, and the life most of the laity lead, makes that difficult, if not impossible. I don't think church leaders and teachers realize that.

I've been reading Hans Küng's book *Judaism* and am impressed with the prodigious scholarship and intense intelligence which goes into it. What a pity that Hans is cut off from so much of the church, as much by theological envy as by papal intolerance. The Jewish people continue to be a mystery to me. How do they fit into Your plan? They are and always have been Your chosen people, a fate for which they have paid an enormous price. To say they rejected Your Son is simply not true.

At least we're not calling them "perfidious" anymore, which is great progress. But anti-Jewishism (as Küng appropriately calls it) still persists and is still terrible to behold. Keep me free, I beg You, from whatever foolish remnants may haunt my personality without my knowing about it. I'll try to work something of that into my sermon tomorrow. But I still wonder why so many don't hear Your self-disclosure in Jesus. It is partly Christianity's fault, because very early on it missed the point of the message and fixated on the messenger. Whether Your Son is the messiah or not is of minor moment compared to the wonder of Your love, which he came to reveal.

We Christians don't hear the message either.

And how could that happen?

One of the great all-time misunderstandings of human history.

April 19, 1992, Easter Sunday — Chicago

My Love,

The Mass at St. Mary's this morning was great fun. My bunny and my Fanny Mae Easter eggs were a hit with the kids and my story about the Generosity Stone was a success with the adults. It's hot and humid and I was pretty well worn out at the end of a very active hour. So I didn't quite get the emotional lift which the Easter Liturgy usually produces. But this festival of spring, this festival of life, is not about emotion but about generosity in response to Your generosity. I hope to write some poetry this afternoon to suit the day, my mood, my weariness, the weather, and the Great Holy Week Flood which has disrupted our city. Fortunately the leak is pretty well plugged by now, for which many thanks.

I finished Küng's book on Judaism, yesterday. It's an impressive piece of work. The only major problem I have with the book is that in his discussion of the Holocaust he rejects the possibility of an explanation from natural theology (theodicy as he calls it). He says one can choose between the immutability of God and the compassion of God. So we must just trust in You. One cannot say, he argues, that You suffer with us. In pastoral practice, one has to appeal either to Your immutability or Your compassion when talking to people about suffering. There isn't much doubt which way to go, not in my mind. His response of trust won't fly with ordinary people, who want to know *why* to trust. The only answer, as far as I know, is that God understands because God suffers with us.

Hans replies that God is, after all, God and can't be weak and vulnerable. Yeah? Then why bother with us at all? It seems to be that, as You are presented in the prophets and in Jesus You want us to understand that You *are* vulnerable, You do need us, You do suffer with us.

So it seems to me that what You are trying to show us in this festival of Life and Love is that You do suffer with us, *insofar as You can*. That seems to fend off Hans's charges that we're trying to make You something less than God.

Ah, but what does that italicized phase mean? Is it not a kind of cop-out? You bet, but it's where I want to put the mystery, where it helps with people to put the mystery, and where I think You want to put the mystery.

Anyway, thanks for Your love and for this spring festival of that love. And of life — life superabundant!

April 20, 1992 — Chicago

My Love,

The smell of Easter lilies in the apartment is a powerful reminder of the season. Like evergreens at Christmas — and mums
in a funeral home. Thank You for that wonderfully... fertile, is
the only word which comes to mind... smell. The smell of Easter
is wonderful, as is everything else about this festival. Yesterday
there were a lot of kids around, at Mass and especially at the
parties: Andrew and Neil Montague, Christine and Katie Durkin,
the very new Nora Grace Gobelbecker, my five grandnieces and
grandnephews. The future, the life, superabundant life which
keeps us going even though our generation will not be around
all that much longer.

In one of the poems I read over the weekend Louis MacNeice
prays for his daughter that she be protected from knowledge of
the suffering which will befall her in her life. In some ways it is
an absurd prayer, yet I understand the sentiment as I hold the
tiny ones in my hands and joke with the not-so-tiny ones. I've
seen enough children grow up and suffer the tragedies of the
human condition. I see their dead bodies in newspaper and TV
pictures or their pinched and hungry faces. So much fierce love
of children and so much tragedy.

What more can I do but pray for all children and ask You to
take care of them, and to pray especially for those that I love the
most, knowing that the tragic dimension of the human condition
cannot be avoided, but neither can its glorious dimension.

The young ones are nonetheless the future. They will remember me as only a vague image from their childhood as they live at
least into the first half of the next century.

I must not cling to life but must with good cheer wish them
well and commend them and their generation to Your care and
protection and love.

April 21, 1992 — Chicago

My Love,

The Cubs won the night game last night, 8–3; I enjoyed it just as I did last year. For that many thanks. It helped to slow me down. It was fun.

As I read MacNeice's poetry, I am impressed by how much the world of nature is sacramental for us. When I see the red tulips on Michigan Avenue on a gray and misty day, I am struck by the contrast and the suggestion of hope and death in combat. If I wasn't rushing through life so quickly I suppose I should see more of those sacraments, those messages from You hinting about what life means.

I love You. Thank You.

April 22, 1992 — Chicago

My Love,

Am I more tired now than I used to be? During the Coleman-Becker seminar last night I almost fell asleep. Is there something wrong with me physically? Or am I growing old?

Of course I'm growing old. How can I deny it. I can't expect to have the energy I had ten years ago, to say nothing of twenty or thirty years ago. Yet I make the same demands on myself as I did then, if not more.

What do I conclude from all of this, my Love?

Well, one of the things I conclude is that it would be awfully nice if You turned the sun on again. I've been back from Arizona for almost six weeks and there has hardly been a single sunny day. Given what I am, that tires me out more than almost anything else.

It's hard to be enthusiastic about religion or love or even You when one is tired, discouraged, and the sun is not shining. It was so nice for the hour or so that You turned it on yesterday afternoon.

I am babbling, that I admit, because I don't have much else to say this morning except that I love You and wish I had more energy on this gray and gloomy day in April.

April 23, 1992 — Chicago

My Love,

I did not mention yesterday the lunch which was most interesting. This was the first sign I have had from anyone over there that they think perhaps they might have made a mistake. Perhaps we have turned a corner. I think You're working overtime on this one. I don't think I'll get any credit from anyone if this all works out in the end, but I don't care. What counts is that justice be done and the church and the priesthood be spared any further disastrous scandal. Grant that it may all work out and soon.

April 24, 1992 — Chicago

My Love,

Another gloomy, damp, drab, morose day — made worse by the clanging phone. My morale is slumping and will, I fear, continue to slump until You turn the sun back on.

I was going to read all day to steady my nerves, but I must go off to an informal lunch to honor the mayor's fiftieth birthday. It shows how morose I am that I use the word "must."

We had a phone call yesterday about the possibility of a TV series. I dusted off the old proposal for a series about the parish in *The Cardinal Virtues* and sent it off. As You know I have not asked You for much in the way of special help in my career as a writer (though I welcome thankfully all the unsolicited help You have given). But on this one I am going to beseech You for assistance. I do really want that series about a contemporary Catholic parish. I can think of no better way to get our message and our image across than such a series. It is the most vivid and most effective medium available.

Please let the sun shine again. I love You, sun or no sun.

April 27, 1992 — Chicago

The sun is supposed to appear today, though shyly and tentatively, like a relative who has been away for a long time. It has been two weeks since she's been with us, according to the weather person last night, so she has every reason to be shy and indeed ought to have some kind of explanation for where she's been and why.

Moreover her return is still problematic. Maybe we'll have her for two days and after that rain and that terrible half-truth "partly sunny," which is the same thing as the "partly cloudy" of my childhood.

Anyway it will be nice to see her again, and when she does show up I promise I will think of You of whom she's a hint and a sacrament.

I continue to be dry and chill, though the poems I've been reading (from the book Jack Shea sent me of poems by women) are enough to thaw almost anyone. Women are not only better novelists than we are because of their skill at detail; they are also better poets because they can express the feelings of love with such exquisite detail.

April 28, 1992 — Chicago

My Love,

She's back! The sun I mean. And clear blue sky! With only a touch of pollution out over the southern end of the lake. Of course it's bitter cold, record cold in fact, and it's going to rain tomorrow. But I promise You gratitude for the return of the sun and I do indeed discharge my debt. The next thing I'd like is spring. Please.

I read some more of the women's poems this morning. Sometimes love is free, says one of them, and sometimes it is costly. Surely that is the case not merely as a general principle but also as a description of any relationship — including a relationship with You. Sometimes You shower me with blessings. Other times You demand everything from me. On the whole I'm the winner because I keep the blessings (most of them at any rate) without giving adequate thanks and don't give everything of myself when You want me to.

I don't do these things maliciously, mind You. Nor am I defending this strategy. I'm merely describing my own behavior, for which I am sorry, though I must add that it is the behavior of every lover, every human lover that is.

"I am filled with God's love," Anne Sexton says in one of her poems. Oh, yes, that is surely true. So am I, both directly and indirectly, though I perceive You only indirectly through all the human loves, many of which I neglect too.

I'm sorry for my failures in love, both direct and indirect. Help me to do better.

Most of my failures are because I rush so quickly through life, just as I am doing at this moment, in a rush to get out to a breakfast meeting. I hope You understand my rushing and forgive me for it. I'll try not to rush so much. But there are so many things to do.

For instance, I talked to the TV people yesterday and then saw the movie *The Player* with Shea in the afternoon. Nice combination. I'm reduced to pitching stories. Well, I'll do that because I want to tell stories on film, and have always wanted to do so, but I won't hold out too much hope that anything will come of it. Yet I do ask You again, grant that this TV series might eventually become a reality.

And thank You much for bringing the sun back!

April 29, 1992 — Chicago

My Love,

The sun continues to shine, wondrous to report, and I already feel better. I understand that my sensitivity to light is part of a whole package, which is surely a welcome package in most respects, and I'll accept the disadvantages without complaint. I guess I need, however, to be patient with myself when the combination of darkness and rush seems to dry me up and make me dull and insensitive to grace.

The time between now and May 10 is going to be rushed with the Irish TV and the talk in New Orleans and Sean's wedding. Then the world should slow down a bit and the transition to Grand Beach begin, a change which I am eagerly anticipating, though, as always, there will be the obligations dragging me back here.

So many obligations, so many things I have to do, so many people eating away at my time and peace.

That's perhaps a *cri de coeur* of which I ought to be ashamed, but it expresses the way I feel when I look at my calendar and consider my life. People demanding time from me without much thought of what the cumulation of these demands do to me.

Well, I've complained enough. I offer You these next two weeks. Help me to be cheerful and faithful through them.

April 30, 1992 — Chicago

My Love,

The end of a very difficult day, class and then wandering about the city with the Irish TV people. The project goes well, but I am very tired from it and the class in combination. It is going to continue to be difficult till Monday and indeed till I leave on Tuesday. Help me, please. When I got back here to the apartment this afternoon I was so tired I could hardly think.

Terrible riots in Los Angeles after the Rodney King acquittal yesterday. America continues to pay a heavy price for slavery. Grant that the riots not spread to other cities. And grant that some way may be found out of the mess of racism and racial injustice.

I'm so tired that I think I'd better go to bed now. I love You.

May 1992

May 1, 1992 — Chicago

My Love,

Saturday morning and a few hours of quiet before the day begins with another rush — film crew, Mass, dinner. As the psalmist says today if I had the wings of a dove I'd fly away to the desert and hide from it all. What does it all matter? What does it accomplish? Why do I bother? What is the point in it all?

Life has so many disappointments. The women's poems I read this morning are heartrending; they are about the loss of a child as the child grows up and sometimes the phenomenon of the child becoming an enemy. Sometimes the child demands independence too soon or too completely or too brutally. Sometimes the mother clings to power too long, too compulsively, too hatefully. I have watched it many times and never understood it, particularly when the conflict is mother/daughter. The poems help me to see the pain of loss for mothers, even when they free their children to be themselves. But seeing the pain does not mean understanding it. Perhaps it is not to be understood.

Particularly at times of weddings do mothers behave, to use a neutral word, oddly. The unconscious and preconscious agenda at these times is often miles deep. Again I don't understand it, but I can at least perceive the pain.

I wonder as I read these poems whether that part of motherhood can apply to You too. In some sense it must; You give us life as mothers do, You bestow on us freedom as mothers do, You watch us grow up and make mistakes as mothers do. How could it not be that You feel loss and pain, insofar as God can, at our errors and tragedies, at our self-inflicted wounds, at our loneliness and frustrations.

It is not easy being a mother, I conclude on this week before Mother's Day. And I can almost hear You say, "Tell me about it!"

May 3, 1992 — Chicago

My Love,

I've been reading David Tracy's new book with considerable profit, particularly the dialogue with Buddhists. Their approach is so foreign to my way of thought. They would be horrified, I think, by this intimate dialogue I am purporting to have with You. So would my fellow Catholic Meister Eckhart, who was searching for the God beyond the Godhead.

My approach, based on Incarnation and analogy, looks almost superstitious and certainly archaic by their standards. How dare one address the totality, the Nothingness, as a lover, as an intimate, as a spouse! Ought I not to let go of my "possessive self" and stop clinging to my own ego by pretending to dialogue with a "thou" who is a "Thou"?

Perhaps.

But, as You might have guessed, I don't think so.

There are many ways of communing with Love, and each to his own way. My interpersonal way is certainly the best for me. In love one does not seek to possess the self but to be possessed (by love itself). One does not cling to existence so much as exist for the other. Admittedly my love affair with You is not yet of that sort, not totally, not even all that much partially, but it is what I want and what I strive for, however imperfectly. Moreover I think this style is more appealing to ordinary people and not just in the West either.

They want a "thou" who is something more than nothing.

It does not follow, however, that one should not worry about clinging too much.

As I will do this crazy week ahead of me, as much as I don't want to.

Take care of me during the plane flights and the confusions. I love You.

May 4, 1992 — Chicago

My Love,
   Another busy day. I'm getting to prayer late at night when I'm tired. The visit to the doctor went well. I continue to have my health, for which I am most grateful to You — even if I put on five pounds since Palm Sunday.
   Tomorrow is my thirty-eighth anniversary to the priesthood and I'll spend it as I spend so much of my time, on a plane, this time to New Orleans. I never would have expected that in 1954.
   Yesterday I went to the First Communion of my friend Maura Anzia. It brought back many memories of my own First Communion fifty-seven years ago. Can it be so long? That little boy in the home movies, so serious and devout, am I he? Yes, of course, still driven by the same energies; I almost said the same demons except I'd like to think they are the same angels. I've tried, heaven knows, since 1935. Maybe that's the whole problem — I've tried too hard, tried as though it all depended on me, or most of it at any rate. I have not yielded enough to You, not even then. Here I can perhaps learn something from David Tracy's Buddhists. Maybe in the few years I have left to me, however many or few they may be, I will learn to trust more in You and to realize that all my hard work is not all that important and my acceptance of Your love is all that really counts.
   Help me to know and to love.

May 6, 1992 — New Orleans

My Love,
   It's a wonderful day in New Orleans, clean, sunny, cool. Not in my experience typical N.O. weather. I had dinner with Jason and his family last night — a wonderful Cajun meal cooked by a woman who is a restaurant critic for one of the local papers. It was a wonderful celebration of my thirty-eighth anniversary.

In a few minutes I'll be leaving for the airport to return to Chicago for the celebration tonight. Thank You for moving me to have these celebrations. One should, I think, celebrate every good thing and each new year in the priesthood is a good thing, very good indeed.

I gave my "God in the Movies" talk today. I'm not sure the fundamentalists in the crowd appreciated my suggestion that You are like Jessica Lange and Audrey Hepburn (though You definitely are!), but I gave them something to think about anyway.

Again I want to thank You for all the wonders and surprises in my years in the priesthood; they have been so many and so spectacular and I don't deserve any of them. It has been a happy and exciting priesthood beyond all my expectations. I'm sufficiently Irish to fear that it might all be taken away or that I'll have to pay for my good fortune. But that's a crazy way to regard human tragedy and human mortality. Surprise and gratitude are the only appropriate responses.

Protect all priests celebrating their anniversaries this year. Some of them have not been as fortunate as I. I know You love them too. Take care of them and renew their hope and their courage and their zeal and their faith.

I love You always, but am especially aware of it on these days of commemoration.

May 9, 1992 — Chicago

My Love,

My friend Bishop Eamonn Casey has resigned as bishop of Galway to become a missionary in South America because of a revelation of a love affair he had nineteen years ago. He is, of course, responsible for his actions. The anger of the woman (which I do not say is unjustified), the hunger of the Irish media for scandal, and the bitter fight about abortion in Ireland now also contributed to the destruction of the man who, as the Irish consul said to me the other night, is the best bishop in Ireland.

The woman said she revealed the love affair (and the existence of a handsome son born of it) because of the hypocrisy of the bishop on celibacy, birth control, and other sexual issues. Granting her sincerity, she waited a long time to do so. It would have been better perhaps to say that she felt she was used and then cast aside, which might be closer to her real feelings. I must leave it to You and the courts of heaven to sort it all out. I do know that we lose one of the best bishops in the world.

At least he wasn't playing with little boys!

It will hurt the church, people say to me, as though Eamonn was the first bishop ever to have a lover. It proves celibacy is wrong, others say, as if infidelity could prove that marriage was wrong. It proves that priests are human and have been from the beginning, but that is all that it proves.

And it is very sad and very tragic for all concerned, the child, the woman, the bishop, the church, and Ireland.

But perhaps it is also Eamonn's salvation.

My thoughts, as You can tell, are random and disorganized and not a little angry. I don't like Greek tragedies, including the ones going on here in Chicago.

Take care of all of them, I beg You.

May 10, 1992 — Chicago

My Love,

I went for a walk yesterday afternoon in the lovely spring weather — tulips, daffodils, young lovers, old lovers, dogs, kids of all sizes and ages — each a manifestation of vitality that You provide on a May Sunday in Chicago. It made me feel strangely sad.

Whence this sadness? Was it mere weariness from two plane flights in a week? Was it the terrible rushing since I returned from Tucson? Was it mortality? Was it a sense of tragedy which haunts the lives of many of the people whose paths I crossed?

To tell the truth I don't know.

But it was unbearable.

Nor do I understand why it came yesterday. Do all the signs of life and vitality seem a lie because death will scrub them out? Well, yes, it will, but I believe in the triumph of life over death, of Easter over Good Friday, don't I? Why so gloomy then? Why so sad?

Was it a Sunday sadness that comes when I slow down from work and have a chance to think about how foolish all my work is? Maybe.

I have more reason to be happy now than I have for years — the appointment at the university, reconciliation with the cardinal, acceptance wherever I go, knowledge that I'm doing a good job. None of it seems to matter anymore.

I don't get it, but it worries me.

Moreover, I think this sadness lurks beneath the surface most of the time. It just came out yesterday because of a concatenation of circumstances.

My faith in You and my love for You seem hypocritical in the face of all this *weltschmertz* — world sadness. That's what it is and myself not even a German.

Yet I am able to keep up the front of the charming, pleasant, witty Irishman even more than I have been in the past.

I know not what to make of this. Maybe I need to write some poetry, though having read Heaney pretty intensively in the last few days, I am ashamed of the inadequacies of my own poetry.

But that's no excuse is it?

So tomorrow for this period of reflection I'll try to capture what happened yesterday and bring my sadness to the surface through metaphors.

Help me.

May 12, 1992 — Chicago

GOLD COAST ON A SUNDAY IN SPRING

Today the Gold Coast is dense with tulips
Deep red and pale white on smooth green beds
And daffodils, snooty dogs, bobbing kids,
The pale skin of lovers still winter white
Absorbs, oblivious, springtime warmth —
An explosion of death-defying vitality
As flowering trees erupt in delicate rage
And young breasts burst against thin cotton blouses

As I watch I am torn by heart-wrenching pain
The rite of spring seems today a foolish dance
A transient ritual of renewal
A charade which fools everyone but death
It is folly and, yes, all is folly
Yet hope undaunted will not go away

May 13, 1992 — Chicago

My Love,

Still running. I'm not going to Grand Beach this weekend, because time has eroded on both sides. But I'll extend my time the weekend after next. Run, run, run.

My class is edifying. The kids really do believe and are really searching for belief. I'm so lucky to be born into and protected by the Catholic tradition. I wish I had more in the way of faith to show for all You've given me.

I feel hollow at times like this, like a machine which keeps on performing — smiling, charming along — while the gasoline in the engine runs dry.

I'll try to spend the weekend slowing down a bit, reading, and maybe revising that poem. Except that I have dinners two of the three nights. Anyway, I love You.

Help me.

May 14, 1992 — Chicago

My Love,

It's noon now, almost a half hour since I began this reflection. This was to be a day of peace at home. As it is I've been on the phone all morning, much of it on the pedophile mess. No rest at all. Moreover I feel dead and empty spiritually from all the running and rushing and being hassled. Maybe I should have gone to the lake today. After I swim I'm going outside for a walk and perhaps to see a movie, though those two escapes aren't as effective as they used to be. I have started a new novel but so far have had no time to get beyond a few paragraphs and have yet to feel much enthusiasm about it. It's hard to work when you are beat out like I am.

Last night the Symphony did Haydn's *Seasons,* which was wonderful. Much romantic music and poetry about spring and summer (we left before fall and winter) and a marvelous young soprano, with Sir Georg conducting (at seventy-nine). I recognized the beauty and the emotion, but they kind of rolled right over me. I am really dry spiritually. I'm afraid I will be till I get away from Chicago, which I will do after lunch next Thursday.

This time is truly bad, not in the external world, where things have been much worse, but in the world of my head, simply worn out by all the demands.

If I were a pastor I could escape the demands by retiring, which many of them are doing long before it is time. But from my responsibilities I can't retire.

Help me, please.

May 15, 1992 — Chicago

My Love,

Eamonn Casey called me yesterday. From a Trappist monastery somewhere. Probably in America but it sounded like an overseas call. Three to six months there, he said. Things quieting down in Ireland. The media still trying to stir things up. I told him that I thought him a fine bishop and a fine priest and nothing would change that position, and I would say it on the public record. He said that he had wanted to tell me about the problem when he came to Grand Beach last summer but couldn't bring himself to do so. Someone to whom I confided about the call said that the bishop must think me important in this life even to bother with the call. I would not have thought that I mattered that much. Wrong again.

Ironically I was reading in St. Luke this morning about Jesus' denunciation of the Scribes and Pharisees for hypocrisy. The same words could be applied to many if not most of our hierarchy today, men who are more interested in their position and power and favor in Rome than they are in either the gospel or their own people. I do not excuse Eamonn's fall from grace, but

I am convinced that the much worse sin is pretending that the world is what Rome wants it to be instead of what it is. That is a much bigger and more damaging lie — more damaging to the church, to religion, and to the gospel.

I am much better today after a good night's sleep and an afternoon of relative peace. Last night I thought I was going to die and rather soon, so tired was I. Today the world looks much better. I have the feeling of one who is beginning to emerge from the cave, and that I will emerge completely in less than a week at Grand Beach.

I love You. Help me out of this cave of rushing and running through darkness.

May 16, 1992 — Chicago

My Love,

Such a beautiful time of the year, especially with the tulips and the flowering trees. And what an awful time for me to be in an exhausted funk. I feel so ungrateful because I barely noticed the crabapples and the lilacs. I'm sorry. I don't mean it to be that way. I'm better now, at least a little bit. It was the two plane trips last week which did me in, I guess. Only a few more days to get to Grand Beach. There is a lot of work to be done up there straightening out the mess. But that waits till next week. This weekend is pure collapse.

I've been reading Mircea Eliade's *History of Religious Ideas* this weekend and am impressed at the incredible variety of ways in which the species has tried to honor You and to account for You and Your ways with us. I guess I can understand the "divinity school mentality" as explained by one of my students the other day. An impersonal God who doesn't much care about us is a lot easier to cope with than a personal God who does care. It is interesting to see how You emerged as Yahweh, not a single new metaphor, Mircea says, yet a whole new religious sensibility. And still very much with us. Moreover likely to remain with us long after the divinity school types are gone.

Sure, our anthropomorphic metaphors are inadequate, but as

I so often say they are inadequate by defect and not excess. That You are Love understates the case.

If only the notion that You are Love would transform my life the way it ought. Then perhaps, even when I'm exhausted and battered, I would have something to cling to before I went under.

I can hardly wait to get to Grand Beach. Life will be easier there. It will, it will, it will.

Help me to love You more.

May 17, 1992 — Chicago

My Love,

I still feel dry and empty though I am no longer particularly tired. I've done my spiritual reading this morning and the only thought I can reflect on is St. Luke's account of the conspiracy to "get" Jesus by the Sanhedrin, a plausible enough narrative because Jesus was pretty clearly a threat to their religious and political power, or so they perceived him. In fact, Jesus wasn't interested in power, but those who have power cannot comprehend such an attitude.

I can understand a little of what went on, and here I begin to reflect on my own situation, because people have been out to "get" me for a long time. I've never been able to understand the animosity of the Catholic intellectual power elite, or the "clerical culture" elite, often represented by ex-priests. Why do they perceive me as a threat to them? I am not comparing myself to Your Son, as I'm sure You understand, but only seeking some consolation in the fact that I'm not the first nor the last to be targeted by hatred.

Yet I'm still baffled by all the animosity. Why should anyone bother? Why should I become an obsession, as I have, for some folks? Why waste energy hating me? Why take such delight in trying to do me in? I am not worth all that effort.

I think I have become somewhat more mellow on the subject. I admit that I've overreacted in the past, and for that I'm sorry.

I'm also sorry that at a time when the night air is such an exquisite sacrament that I have nothing more to say.

May 18, 1992 — Chicago

My Love,

At supper last night a lot of serious talk about some problems among my friends. It was a useful conversation in the sense that it helped me understand what was happening, but it didn't give me any notion of what could be done. Nothing most likely. How often in the human condition that is the case. People get themselves in such troubles, mess up things so badly, and then become prisoners of their own bad decisions. How much of the tragedy of human life results from bad things we do to ourselves that we are not really forced to do, from mistakes that ought not to have been made, from errors in judgment that are hardly reasonable.

It is easy after a discussion like that to be troubled and to wonder whether the human condition offers much hope. In my novels hope for change and rebirth always triumphs. Sometimes it does in the real world too — consider William Kennedy's mad happy ending in *Very Old Bones*. I don't say that happy ending stories are weak (as some movie critics and book reviewers would have us believe.) I merely say that in the real world they are infrequent.

I don't believe You want it that way. And I do believe that You want novels like mine to offer people the possibilities of change and happiness. But when I see some of the things I've seen this spring (You know what I mean) and note how people create senseless unhappiness for themselves, I wonder about how far away we are from what Father Teilhard called *le point Omega*.

Hell of a long way, it seems to me.

More on the pedophile mess today and tomorrow. It continues to be a Greek tragedy.

Help me to see this one through successfully. I love You.

May 19, 1992 — Chicago

My Love,

The state's attorney called me yesterday, just as I was about to leave for Barry Moriarity's twenty-fifth anniversary Mass; he is apparently willing to talk directly with some of the pedophile victims' families. That could be an opening which might lead to a turnaround. I hope so. I also would like desperately to get out from under this problem. It is consuming time and energy and emotions, and I'd like to be free of it. However, I'm the only priest in town with the freedom to be able to write and speak out about the subject, and maybe something good will come of it. Please grant for the sake of the families that this opening might prove a breakthrough.

Barry's Mass was wonderful! He is truly a remarkable priest, all the best of the South Side Irish incarnated in one wise and witty man. The mayor was at my table, looking incredibly young and fit, apparently rejuvenated by his three-day fishing trip. I wish rejuvenation was always as easy as catching a fish. Tomorrow after class I leave for Grand Beach. That will be so wonderful. I truly can hardly wait. Help me to really relax this time. I love You. Help me to love You more.

May 21, 1992 — Grand Beach

My Love,

It is so wonderful to be here! The sweetness of Grand Beach in my life becomes more important each year. I don't think I've ever been so tired at the beginning of summer — and that's without any European trip. There's stuff to be done to get organized but I'm not going to do much this weekend. Just loaf and read.

This must all be boring to You. Having read my journals I know how tired I am when I get up here, how much I complain about this in my reflections, and how poorly I do in the relaxation business. Help me to truly relax this summer, to shake off the demands and the burdens and become close to You.

I love You.

May 24, 1992 — Grand Beach

My Love,

Memorial day is a strange combination of life and death. We put out our flowers (which I have done, and by the way many thanks for the rain right after I got the last of the impatiens in!) to celebrate the beginning of summer (and in this part of the world perhaps the arrival of a sudden and brief spring), and yet we also use the flowers to decorate graves, especially of those who died during the wars our country has fought. We remember all the young men and women who looked forward to the beginning of summer and yet never lived to see it. And by extension some of us remember all our dead. While the Irish aren't great for it, other ethnic groups swarm out to the cemeteries to decorate graves and be with their dead, even eat picnics with them. I used to think such customs were ridiculous, but as I've grown to better understood religious metaphors, I am much more tolerant. There is a rich sense of "Communion of Saints" in such actions, though they are not necessarily everyone's cup of tea.

Have I ever been to my parents' grave since my mother died thirty years ago? I don't think so. Does it follow that I don't miss them or love them enough? No way. Perhaps it is a too literal response to Your Son's dictum, "Let the dead bury the dead." Or maybe it is resurrection faith. Or maybe it is Irish suppression of grief. Whatever, does it leave a little bit to be desired? I'll have to ponder that.

I think I approach this summer in somewhat better physical shape than other summers and perhaps in rather poor psychological shape because of the demands of the last two months. I thank You — oh, how much I thank You! — for this place of refuge, one of Your more important gifts to me. Help me to make good use of it this summer! I love You!

May 25, 1992 — Grand Beach

My Love,

You surely changed the Memorial Day Weekend yesterday when You sent the weather front through which plunged the temperature 40 degrees by night. I'm not sure whether I should be crediting You with the weather. On the one hand, why should You be concerned about a holiday on a tiny cosmic speck and with the laws of nature on that speck which You established when You launched it into existence. On the other hand, since I believe You lurk everywhere and that You love all of us on this cosmic speck I can't fall back on the Deist notion that You're not here in the weather because You have other things do.

You're involved with us. That much I know.

In my spiritual reading this summer, I'm going to concentrate on contemplation (if that combination of "c" words is not a contradiction). There is so much to contemplate. Rather than being immune to the glories of creation here on the lake side (or anywhere else) I am overwhelmed by them — and tend to rush by them because somehow there isn't time for all of them and it seems unfair to spend time on only one. I realize that sounds zany, but it's the way I seem to work. A day without a schedule, even on a relaxed weekend like this, somehow seems to be an imperfect day, a day in which I might not accomplish anything.

In one sense the efficiency with which I work is a grace; it enables me to accomplish a lot, I hope in Your service. On the other it dries me up and leaves me worn and empty. Well, here at the beginning of the summer I promise I'm going to try to do better — "to see" — and beg You to help me.

In the collection of "experiential" poems I am reading up here, I came this morning upon Keats and "The Nightingale." Somehow he resonates with my sense today of the almost unbearable beauty of the world in which You have put us. Help me to face this unbearable beauty during the summer and see You in it.

Why unbearable? I think because of the fleeting time we have to rejoice in it. But I'll return to that subject tomorrow.

May 26, 1992 — Grand Beach

My Love,

In reading Abbot Thomas Keating this morning I learned again that contemplation is letting go of the conscious self (which is, in part, the false self) and freeing up the unconscious or the preconscious, as I would call it.

My preconscious, as we both know, works feverishly when I'm before the computer. Maybe my Compaq is the key to unlocking my own contemplative dimension. That this would be an unusual approach I freely acknowledge. But that doesn't make it wrong, not since You made us all so different, one from another. Might it be self-serving and self-deceptive? Sure it might; any form of prayer might be, so I cannot reject the possibility on those grounds only. The one objection to this theory is that my reflections here, while under the influence of my preconscious as all my writing is, comes out cognitive and propositional. I write poems, stories, and prose. This prayer is always prosaic, rational, discursive. I don't think You would reject it for that reason; in fact, I'm sure You would not. But to let my contemplative self work, it perhaps should be a mix of prose and poetry. In other words, I should let imagery flourish. You can understand my images as well as my sentences. The trouble with trying to write poetry in these reflections is that I tend to spend a lot of time on form and meter and rhythm.That's not what is required in these reflections. Rather it should be raw and spontaneous imagery, perhaps at the beginning of the reflections. Perhaps through all of the reflections some days.

I will try that tomorrow, starting with Wordsworth's image of having already crossed the Alps, which I read today.

I love You.

May 30, 1992 — Grand Beach

My Love,

Tired, tired, tired. I'm sorry. A few days in Chicago destroyed me. New work piled on. Not much contemplation possible. Help me. I love You.

May 31, 1992 — Grand Beach

My Love,

I've finished the three essays, which suddenly became an obligation last week, and am ready now for vacation and must instead return to Chicago for four busy and hellish days before I come back here. I'm still heavy and dry, much too busy about too many things. I feel used, exploited, pushed, battered. I want to do only one of the things which are to happen between now and

Thursday. The rest are obligations, "have tos" instead of "want tos." I'm grumpy ("No kidding!" You say), crabby, and impatient. I merely want to be left alone. I don't want to go to any dinners, talk to any reporters, put on any public performances. When I get back here I'll have only the novel to work on, and that is fun compared to all the rest of the junk.

Pretty much of a mess, huh?

I've permitted the run-up to my vacation to be destroyed, in good causes I admit, but destroyed just the same, and for that I'm sorry. Help me to snap out of the funk I'm in, to stop complaining and feeling sorry for myself. Thank You.

I love You.

June 1992

June 3, 1992 — Chicago

My Love,

I'm reading Harold Bloom's book on American religion. He says that religion is a search for meaning in the face of meaninglessness, an attempt to persuade ourselves that we do not die. In a certain sense he is right, though he obviously sees religion — and our postulation of You — as a form of wish fulfillment. It would be very nice indeed if You exist because then our lives wouldn't be completely meaningless and in some sense we wouldn't die. Therefore we believe these things so that we don't have to live in the midst of meaninglessness.

However, that we wish something to be true does not make it false either! One doesn't disprove religion by arguing that we *wish* it were so. Of course we wish it were so, but whether it is so or not remains to be seen, and the fact that we'd like it to be true proves nothing one way or another.

Bloom is the kind of atheist — or gnostic as he calls himself — who thinks that tough-mindedness is a proof of superior courage. But it might just as well be a proof of existential insensitivity.

However — and this is the point of my reflection — the thought that there might be no meaning at all is terrifying. I don't have all that many years left, maybe not many at all. Has all my work been a waste? Is it all chaos? Do I exist between two oblivions?

I don't think so. I do believe in You, and I think it is as hard-headed to believe as not to believe, perhaps more so. I believe in love, *Love,* rather than chaos, but as Wellington said at Water-loo, it's a damn near thing. Or, to put it differently, a little terror is not at all a bad thing. Faith without occasional terror is cheap grace.

But protect me from too much terror!

June 4, 1992 — Chicago

My Love,

As I read the women's poetry this morning I am impressed by the anger in so much of what they write. It's often hard to see who the object of their anger is; usually it is their parents or their husband (ex-husband generally), sometimes their children. I wonder if this goes with the condition of being a woman or whether it is peculiar to women poets. Or is it merely poets in general? Or humans in general? How often does a feeling of anger or oppression or grievance become the matrix of our life, the warp and woof of our existence? How often do we define ourselves over against our enemies? We *are* in opposition to our enemies. Bad business!

Nor am I immune from this propensity. Not for nothing have I been compared to Don Quixote.

Help me to forgive, and to know forgiveness.

I do love You.

June 7, 1992 — Grand Beach

My Love,

Warm sun, clear sky, blue lake, waves against the beach, flowers blooming, the sound of children playing — summer starts today and the discussion about evil, which was appropriate at Mass last night because it was the late Kevin Daley's birthday, begins to fade into the background. And yet, chaos lurks beneath the lake, that melted glacier. How many people have drowned in it — including the Irish seminarian whose body I discovered so many years ago? Rest him and grant him happiness. Danger also simmers in the sun, which can parch fields and infect skin.

Danger on the beach, danger for the kids, danger seems to lurk everywhere.

And the danger of obsession — the overanalysis into which I have stumbled and from which I can't seem to escape. Thinking of another wasted summer, worried about a violation of the covenant by one of Your allies. Help me to understand that unlike most people my temptation is not to be lazy but rather to work too much. Help me slow down and thus order the forces of chaos in my own life.

Well, those are good intentions. I'll work on the novel each day but only do three thousand words and turn off the phone in the morning. Those should be simple tasks and they may also improve the quality of the fiction if I try to do a little every day instead of everything at once.

And thank You for this summer!

June 8, 1992 — Grand Beach

My Love,

Cool, sunny, no breeze quiet lake, beginning to relax, not bad for a Monday. I refuse to rush at anything. Novel in abeyance. Reading Yeats again: mystical, nostalgic, melancholy. So lyrical, so Irish. I am trying in my stories to bring back my own dreams, to make the stories mystical and nostalgic and bittersweet but still hopeful.

All is not lost, not yet. Something can yet be retrieved, not perfectly, but still resurrected and kept alive. Proust was wrong and Joyce was right. Not only can the times lost be found and represented; in a profound Catholic sense they can be relived and this time lived correctly. With Your help I have done it and will continue to do it, both in story and in life.

For that opportunity I am very grateful.

June 9, 1992 — Grand Beach

My Love,

This morning I read three summer poems — Hardy, Thomas, Hopkins. The first two see death. Hardy rather hears it in the bell tolling for a funeral and thinks of it tolling for himself. Thomas sees the hawk kill the sparrows and wonders why You permit it. (So do I, as far as that goes; so does everyone who thinks about the "chain of life.") And Hopkins sees in the summer fields just harvested Your Son and the promise of life without end.

Who is to say that one of the poets is right and the others are wrong? Summer can mean both life and death. The issue is which is stronger. This summer, not quite upon us, promises life, good times, friends, guests, festivals. As it goes along, however, as it slips through my fingers, there will also be a strong hint of death, one last summer.

What will people say of me when I am dead? Probably that I was controversial, that I had friends and enemies, that I did unconventional things, that my sociology was good or at least adequate, that I wrote a lot, that the reviews of my novels were generally unfavorable (not true but let it go), that I was a gadfly, that my fellow priests were ambivalent about me, etc. A reasonably impressive life, I guess, but not all that great.

What will You think? I mean I know You'll always love me, and that's what matters. But will You say that I spread myself out too thin, that I tried to do too much, that I did not permit myself to enjoy all the blessings You gave me, that I was, after all, something of a workaholic and You never approve of that? Will You say I missed out on the important things in life because I was such a willing victim of schedule and obligation? That I was too quick to take offense, too combative, too trusting, and then too untrusting?

Maybe You will. I obsess about changing — whether I should change, whether I can change.

I can't help but continue this reflection, as morose as it is — a kind of anticipated particular judgment.

Help me to know and understand that You love me as You love us all — without judgment.

June 10, 1992 — Grand Beach

My Love,
   No matter how I arrange my days, I don't seem able to get the desk cleared till 3:00. More phone calls and interruptions. Perhaps I should have turned to these reflections before my swim this morning because after that it was 9:30 and open season on me. I still have not turned off the phone because too many things are happening that I must stay on top of. And I continue to struggle with the new novel.
   I have read about St. Cuthbert and giving oneself over to God. To remember similar things and to surrender completely to You means letting go. But, as You well know, none of the matters on my agenda this morning could be so easily dismissed as unimportant. In most of them, I was not the one who stood to gain or lose, nor was I the one who could let go. What is one to do about obligations? Surely casting myself into Your love does not free me of commitments or responsibilities?
   So hard to figure. I'm playing into too many games, obviously. But which games should I abandon?
   Right now, as You well know, I am sleepy, very sleepy indeed. And I have, of course, a grave obligation to watch the Bulls tonight. It is absolutely certain that I must start writing my novel at six or earlier because I cannot write a story and answer the phone at the same time. So weary and confused. I know what the Bulls feel like at the end of a stormy season!

June 11, 1992 — Grand Beach

My Love,
   This morning I read poems by Yeats, Dickinson, and Hopkins, all of them enough to make me wary of ever trying to write a word of verse again!
   Yeats sees death in frustrated love (though I suspect he would have been unhappy if Maud Gonne had actually married him). Dickinson sees death in a certain way the light falls. And the good Jesuit rejects the "carrion comfort" of despair. How wonderfully Catholic of him!

Poets write so much about love and death, joy and frustrated hopes as a prelude to death.

But I guess that's what poetry is supposed to be about. What else do sacrament makers in a species that knows the agony of love and the certainty of death make sacraments about?

There is a convocation of the priests of the archdiocese this week out at a place called Pheasant Run. I excused myself on the grounds that I really haven't been a priest of the archdiocese for a quarter of a century. In fact, I believe I told them not to leave the lights on in my room or to wait up for me, which was perhaps excessive. But not untypical, You say.

I have already talked to You about whether I should have gone and I don't have much doubt about that.

I'm writing a novel now about someone who goes to the junior seminary in my class and leaves after third year. I realize how much part of that world I was and how little part of it I am now. In a way that's not bad because I have a freedom that I would never had if I hadn't become an outcast.

I don't make much of a contribution to the archdiocese either, at least not directly. In the last year I have had at least some influence on it indirectly and, You being willing, might have more. It is also a blessing that the reconciliation with the cardinal came when it did. There's no chance now of my being coopted into the system.

Yet I never chose to be a marginal priest, as I have said to You so many times. I guess I chose to do and say the things that made me marginal, though naively I didn't think they would. I know better now and in a certain sense it is too late to turn back. Even if there were any chance of becoming part of the archdiocese again, my assault on the pedophile problem precludes that. How ironic!

Yet I have many good friends who are priests of the archdiocese and now the class wants me to come to the reunions. Which next year I must do.

You can get so far out that you're in!

What do I conclude?

The most obvious: that You know what You're doing.

And that Hopkins is right, poor dear unhappy man.

June 12, 1992 — Grand Beach

My Love,

   I must drive to Chicago today for the baptism tomorrow and won't be back till Sunday. Unfortunately I will probably have to do the same thing some time next week when the recommendations on pedophilia of the cardinal's commission are released. I pray it's a good report. So much hinges on it. Clearly the press conference will be "solemn high" and very important, with the national media closing in. Unless someone warns them to do it candidly, they'll blow it.

   Today I read Michelangelo and Herbert on the failure of their verse and the closing off (as it seemed to them) of Your love. They equate their poetry with a sense of Your presence. In truth it's been a long time since I've been able to do any verse — since I came back from Dublin. It seems that I write poems best in the melancholy fall. But poetry is not as important in my life as it was in theirs.

   And yet I do believe in metaphor as the only way to talk about You, and my metaphors have not been functioning too well lately. I may need the poetry to be open to Your presence.

   The months since I came home from Tucson (just three months ago today) have been terrible — rush, rush, rush. There was no time for metaphor. I'll try to return to poetry next week and open myself to Your presence within me and all around me.

June 13, 1992 — Chicago

My Love,

   I now must stay two extra days in Chicago because the cardinal's commission on pedophilia will issue its report on Monday, and the media will be all over town looking for me. As best as I can tell, the report will be good though it won't solve the problems in places like Northbrook. I hate to miss Grand Beach on a weekend like this but I guess there's not much choice. Clearly You want me to be around.

   I can work on my novel here tomorrow and Monday just as if I were at Grand Beach and bring it pretty close to half way finished, which is a desirable goal. And I'll go back Monday night a basket case, but that's the way it goes.

I read a wonderful poem by Kathleen Norris this morning about faith and forgiveness in which she deftly reviews the lives of members of her family in ages past. I wish I could write poems like that. Bob McGovern at Ashland Poetry Press wrote that he will indeed publish my own poems in October under the excellent title *The Sense of Love*. I am worried about their adequacy, just as I was worried about my first novel, but you have to take your chances.

I also regret that I don't know more about my own past like Kathleen Norris did, but why not write a novel in which I make all those people come alive in fantasy? That's what I'll do in my next story, the "September" one.

I must now go off to officially welcome into the church a certain Nora Grace, for whom much thanks!

I love You.

June 14, 1992 — Chicago

My Love,

Leo Mahon tells me there was an "ovation" at the priest's convocation when Phil Murnion mentioned my name. I don't doubt that there was some applause, but I can't imagine that there was a lot of it.

It does raise the question again as to whether I ought to reconsider my relationship to the archdiocese. My answer on this hot Sunday morning is still no. There's simply too much animosity over my public stance on the pedophilia crisis for me even to think about it at the present time. To accept a niche back in clerical culture would be a grave mistake; it would mean running the risk of being coopted. You've given me freedom and I do not want to give it back, not for any ovation.

June 15, 1992 — Chicago

My Love,

The Bulls won last night, which cheers me up. Today is the pedophile report release, which may keep me busy much of the day. Tonight I fervently hope I can get back to Grand Beach.

Dear God, I'm so tired. So edgy. I need to be left alone, and I don't know whether that will ever happen. I'm trying to write a novel, which in itself is no great problem, but as in every other novel I've ever written it's the distractions which put me on edge. When I get back to the lake I'm going to try to get on the schedule which enables me to start work at 4:00 A.M. and finish up before the phone and the distractions start.

But that's no way to rest. I should turn off the phone, I really should.

Sorry for the complaining again. I love You. Help me through the day.

June 16, 1992 — Grand Beach

My Love,

This last weekend was a weekend from hell. Today, weather permitting, I will go to the beach. I do not intend to let the end of spring (five days away) slip by without spending some time enjoying the gift that is right in front of my face.

Coleridge's "dejection" was on my reading agenda this morning, a very Victorian lament for lost joy. He says that joy is a gift and we have no right to it. How much joy is there in my life? There was certainly joy in getting back here last night — or was it only relief. There will be joy in getting to the beach this afternoon, but that's not real joy. Am I not dejected most of the time too? Certainly during this terrible weekend.

I know the answer to this problem. I will be able to experience joy, the joy of spring and summer, the joy of peace and reflection only when I am able to give myself time for these things, when I'm able to put aside my responsibilities and my commitments. *I must do it.* I must do it starting today.

Help me. Help me recapture joy, because there is so much in which to rejoice.

June 17, 1992 — Grand Beach

My Love,
   I'm now on the four o'clock schedule and as always it's hard, as least hard to get used to waking up before the sun does. It is, unfortunately, the only way I can get a novel written. It will be better when I can fall asleep at eight at night.
   And I have another long interview on the pedophilia mess this morning. Won't they ever stop? The answer is no they won't, and I have only myself to blame, for getting involved.
   But how can anyone not get involved when children's lives are at stake?
   The poems I read this morning are in one way or another about childhood. As I work on my present novel, I recall my own childhood. How happy a time was it? Very early on it was very happy, as the poets remember their childhoods. By school time it had become less so though the hard times were, I suppose, only in the later years of grammar school. But, without going the whole route with Wordsworth, can I at least see the happiness of early childhood as if a promise of the future? I should like to think it so. The fun-filled little kid, like my grandniece and grand-nephew today, knows perhaps more about what life means than the weary adult.
   I hope that is so. I believe it is so. But this morning I am so tired I can hardly type these words.
   I love You. Help me to be like a child again and reenter the Kingdom of heaven.

June 18, 1992 — Grand Beach

My Love,
   The poems I'm reading all stress going off into the country and seeking Your face in nature. Except that You also lurk in the city and its people — in the rioters and the gang members, the

journalists and the politicians, the priests and the prostitutes, in battered wives and in shattered lives.

I am not protesting against seeking You in nature. You were here in the storm yesterday and in the gold-on-silver color of the lake afterwards. But You are in the cities in a special way. In a sense my escape here in the summer is from the urgency of knowing You in the city.

Again I have become deeply involved in the pedophile crisis only because I see You in the least of the brothers and sisters being brutalized multiple times by the church. This fight has consumed so much time and energy and thought and has given so little payoff in satisfaction. How many phone calls every day!

But it is an obligation, a necessity, something I *must* do no matter how distracting from prayer and other things it is.

I'm too tired this morning to figure it all out, but I know that You are in the city too.

And I love You there as much as I love You here at Grand Beach.

June 19, 1992 — Grand Beach

My Love,

Three press interviews yesterday, two of them over an hour in length. I want to be still and still the phone rings. The only answer is to get out of the house, which I did yesterday afternoon. I keep telling people that I'm on vacation, which is not altogether true. But I should be on vacation except for my novel writing, and yet that doesn't stop the incessant phone.

The interview about prayer was interesting even though I was reluctant to do it. I tried not to pretend that I was more devout than I am or even that I was close to being as devout as I'd like to be. I hope I didn't give the wrong impression. I suppose the most surprising part was that journalist had read the book which contained the first year of these reflections, a book I still can't finish reading myself.

That book gave me great pause, but I have no regrets about publishing it. If it helps someone to pray, then that's all that matters. But I wonder sometimes about the nature of this daily prayer journal and the extent to which my reflections are authentic. I know that I *want* to be talking to You, that I want to be sharing with You my feelings, my affection, my love. I also realize, as I told the reporter, that it's taken me a long time to realize that the kind of prayer which one does best is what one should do and that praying this way is the best way I have found in a long life of distractions.

Yet I still am not sure. I know You're listening. I believe that. But often that belief does not seem to penetrate my consciousness all that much and these prayers seem to be rote reflections done as an obligation before I go on to other obligations.

I don't know. I'm not a very devout person. But I'd like to be. Maybe I don't understand what devotion is. I'm confused by the whole matter. I only know I love You. I know I became a priest to serve You. And I'm afraid that my work may get in the way of that service. I know that it has had a tremendous effect on people. Yet I'm not sure what You think of me.

Isn't that silly? I do know what You think of me. You love me the way any tender lover loves, *only more so*. Despite all my faults.

Nonetheless, I'm uneasy about the faults which these reflections reveal. I don't mind others knowing about them. I mind the faults themselves.

June 20, 1992 — Grand Beach

My Love,

I read a religious magazine this morning. In one of the articles, rambling and narcissistic, was a good line: "It's always necessary to be close to beauty." How true that is, how very true! You've enabled me to surround myself with beauty, both natural and created, in the places where I live and work. The beauty should remind me of You and that is the idea. Sometimes it does. But often it doesn't. As when I go to the symphony and become so distracted by my various projects and preoccupations that I don't even hear the music. Or when I have the stereo on and notice the music only occasionally and even then but rarely relate it to You.

In one sense it is unnecessary to relate the music to You. It has its own sacramental value without my being conscious about it.

But in a larger sense a sacrament of Your love consciously perceived is more powerful as sacrament than one not consciously perceived. So I will make more of an effort to hear You and see You in the music and beauty all around me. I know I've said that often before. But I hope, with Your grace, to keep trying.

And if You can arrange to have summer come on time I'd be pleased too.

June 21, 1992 — Grand Beach

My Love,

"Does not my God deserve the best?" the poet asks this morning. I wonder if I have given You the best. How can one write twenty novels in ten years and still think they're the best he can do? Are they pot-boilers? Many critics think so. Most readers do not. But that I think is not the issue. One does what one can. One writes the way one is able to write. You've given me a specific kind of talent and I must follow it's impulse and spirit. I write what I am able to write. The story that I'm working on now is better than the previous ones. I improve as a writer within my own genre by writing. I ought not to care that it's different from the way other people write, any more than I ought to care that this method of prayer, so terribly useful for me, is different from other people's methods of prayer.

If you're different, you're different. It is Your Spirit which makes me different from others (all of us different from everyone else) and that's the way we ought to be.

I do what I can. And yet it isn't enough. I always want to do better. But I will never deny the direction in which You have sent me, never permit the Spirit to be denied. And I assert as firmly as I can that You *do* deserve the best.

Thank You for the ability to write stories that people like to read. I thank You for all the good things You've given me. Help me to realize how much You love me and need me. Help me to love You a little more in return. And also take care of my nieces and my friend Jack, all of whom have important weeks ahead of them.

June 23, 1992 — Grand Beach

My Love,

In the passage from "In Memoriam," which my book of mystical poetry offers up to me this morning, Tennyson, a classic Victorian romantic if there ever was one, wonders why the Scripture does not tell us what Lazarus saw. Were his lips sealed so he could not describe death? Or was it too much for him to share?

Poor Lord T. didn't know what we know about Scriptures. He didn't realize that was not part of the story the author of St. John's Gospel wanted to tell, that for his era the question was much less important than it is for a much more subjectivist era.

Moreover we don't know whether Lazarus was clinically dead in the modern sense of the term. Surely he was not in heaven and than yanked back, like a fish.

Yet the question is valid after all. What is the world to come like? Someone I ran across the other day described it as "unbelievable," meaning that he didn't believe it. That of course is his faith, just as much as my faith is that life is stronger than death. Either way, the scientific data are inconclusive — though probably the data lean in the direction of survival.

However, the rejection of survival is in effect a commitment to the notion that life and creation are meaningless, a conclusion that humankind in general has always rejected and does so even today. Either life is monstrous or there are grounds for hope. And if there are grounds for hope, then there must be You. Attempts to hedge and fudge just don't work.

Anyway I want to reassert on this sleepy morning at 4:35 A.M. while I strive to finish the novel that I do love You and do believe in You and also do believe that life and love are stronger than death and hate.

June 24, 1992 — Grand Beach

My Love,

I should finish the first draft of the novel today, which will be an enormous relief. Revision remains. I wish I could work on it more than two full days this week and let my other obligations slide. Revision is fun.

Henry Vaughan in the poem I read this morning says that he wishes it were night all the time because at night the world does not distract him from You the way it does during the day. It's a lovely poem, which sees You as more present in darkness than in light. The only trouble is that, given time, we find the distractions in the darkness too — he says at 4:25 A.M. in the glow of his work station. Distractions are not a matter of time of day or position of sun but of style of life. I've been in over my head for decades and the distractions are not things that are all that pretty but rather responsibilities, like the pedophile crisis. Of, on a much lesser note, simply the obligation of everyday life.

I often feel like a machine that other people are running for their own purposes without regard for my own humanity. That's an exaggeration, but one with truth to it. I must admit that I have permitted this to happen.

Help me!

I love You.

June 26, 1992 — Chicago

My Love,

The novel is finished! Thank You! I like it. I hope You do too.

I'm in Chicago in preparation for the wedding tomorrow. I'm so tired. I don't know whether it was wise to work the way I have, but when I'm involved in a story I can't stop. I'm sorry if I've pushed too hard and worked myself too hard. I've been running too hard. I do love You and on this rushing day I wanted to confirm that Love.

June 28, 1992 — Grand Beach

My Love,

The poem this morning contrasts the beauty of summer with the death of children in war. It hit me strongly because of the terrible killing in Bosnia this summer — while the world watches in paralysis as these ancient blood feuds kill thousands. It is all the more horrifying because Sarajevo appears to be a civilized city with men and women in twentieth-century dress, a modern European city.

The same Europe where the Holocaust took place. There is nothing "unmodern" about barbarism — witness the terrible disaster we visited on Iraq. Humans have done and are still doing such terrible things to other humans who are ever so slightly different from them in race or religion.

I wish I could do something, even a little bit, to stop it. Yet I can't, other than perhaps write columns about it, which is just about nothing. I know how the poet felt. Here I am beginning to enjoy summer or at least beginning to get ready to enjoy it, and innocents are dying. It doesn't seem right, yet what can I do.

Do You ask Yourself the same things? Do You wonder what You can do? Or do You weep but plan for the future in some combination that I can't begin to imagine?

I love You. I believe in You.

June 30, 1992 — Grand Beach

My Love,

An image from yesterday: a sparrow lying dead on my pool cover, perhaps having smashed into the picture window. I felt grief for the tiny but determined life which had been snuffed out, even a sense of responsibility because my window had killed him. But then I thought also of the image Your Son used when he was here among us: Not one of them falls without Your concern, a concern for the life of the small creatures which makes mine look trivial and a metaphor for You which astonishes. It surely is a response to the deists and all the others who picture You as the *deus otiosus,* the lazy God who no longer cares about us. Jesus says You care even about the sparrows. It is hard to find anywhere in human religious imagery a picture of You that is quite that powerful. Not only do You know but You *care.* Do I believe that? Dear God, yes, I believe because I want so desperately to believe it. If that image of Jesus is valid then "all will be well and all will be well and all manner of things will be well." Do You really care about the birds of the air? Why is their world such a savage one? Why so much abundance and superabundance of life? Yet You care. Jesus says so, and he knows You better than anyone else has ever known You. Help me to believe it more strongly.

And I'll leave the shutters on to protect Your avian friends in the future.

July 1992

July 1, 1992 — Grand Beach

My Love,

Ah, the first day of summer! I notice so many more events which remind me of You when I have slowed down just a little. I'm off for the Beach as soon as I finish these reflections.

I also want to thank You for the idea of the electronic piano. Oh, my, it is so beautiful! It will bring so much happiness to my guests and to many others long after I'm gone. It will provide me with music for Mass, perhaps, in weeks to come. I'm glad You arranged that Joe Nasser showed it to me and that I was able to buy it. Thank You so much.

Now to my reflections. I watched the movie *Only the Lonely* on TV last night. What a wonderful film, what a wonderfully Catholic film. On four grounds I liked it. First of all, as someone who fell in love with Maureen O'Hara in *The Quiet Man*, it was good for me to see that beauty does survive age and transcends it. Secondly, the movie made me see Chicago again as the incredibly beautiful city that it is, particularly the fairy tale railroad station at Christmas time. I thank You for the beauty of my city and beg You to make it a better place for all to live. Help me to see You lurking in it. Thirdly, the portrait of older love fits perfectly with my sociological report coming out in August, one which will be duly footnoted, an extra point of strength for the report. Finally, the picture of a certain kind of Irish family life was incredibly poignant, very funny. Rarely have I laughed so hard by myself when watching a film. But it was also very sad, because the typical domineering Irish mother is less graceful in defeat than Maureen O'Hara was in the film — sad because so many lives have been ruined by that particular twisted passion for control.

I marvel at how powerful the syndrome is and how persistent even to the present generation. I don't understand it, but I have a horror of it. Our families can truly twist our lives in incredible ways. Is it peculiar to the Irish heritage or do we have a peculiarly virulent form of it because of our culture and our history of survival under oppression?

One of the troubles with it is that the dominating parents (mother usually) suffer as much as the children because they are always disappointed and suffer terribly because of the disappointment. Very, very sad indeed.

I thank You that it hasn't ruined my life, and I pray for those whose lives it has ruined. Help me as a priest and a storyteller to always fight against it.

And thank You for the wonderful film.

July 3, 1992 — Grand Beach

My Love,

Oh God! Book II was weak. The idea of George Burns as You kind of wore out, though there were some wonderful jokes. It suffered from being too cute by half (possibly because there were five script writers). The charm of the first two films was lost. Yet there was nonetheless the picture of You as concerned about Your creatures and eager for their love and attention, a picture which would be blasphemous if it were not for the self-portrait in the Scriptures (in Deuteronomy 32, Hosea 11, Isaiah 36 and 42): a mother who carries us in Her arms and who bends down to nurse us. Those who would reject the tears of God must reject the metaphors of the Scriptures, metaphors which are the basis in their turn for the image of the suffering God in Jesus, Your Son.

For all its cuteness, the George Burns kind of God is more

accurate than most God pictures that we pick up from our philosophy and theology books.

You wept for the mother killed by lightning yesterday. You wept for those pedophile victims on TV last night. You suffer with all those who suffer because You love us like a parent, like a weeping mother.

I love You.

July 7, 1992 — Grand Beach

My Love,

Last night I watched *The Hunt for Red October* and realized how much the world has changed since last summer. Nuclear war is no longer a serious danger. Communism is dead. World peace is a given.

There is indeed terrible conflict in the Balkans and in what used to be the USSR and grave dissatisfaction among the cold war winners (hard to understand). But nonetheless the world has gone through the most important change of the twentieth century and for that much thanks indeed.

Much thanks for the changes in my life too. The cardinal and I are friends again. I'm on the faculty at the university, however marginally. The world is a much better place for me, and I am grateful.

Yet a certain tension remains. I'm trying to juggle so many different values and goals and projects that I'm not sure I trust myself or my motivation. I want to improve my novels, I want to clean up the pedophile mess, see the innocent vindicated, the cardinal protected, the church reformed. All of these are valid goals and not incompatible, but it's hard to keep all my motivations clear and precise. I do my best. I pray for Your help. But I also scheme and connive and plot, like I did (with not altogether happy results) at the time of the [Cardinal] Cody scandal. It makes me nervous. I've got to watch myself every step of the way.

I love You.

July 9, 1992 — Grand Beach

My Love,
   My friend Jack Shea is here so there is much serious talk about
prayer and spirituality and meditation. It makes me realize how
distracted and unfocused my spiritual life is. Oddly enough, in
the mail today I received from Mike Leach [publisher] the first
review of the second volume of these reflections, *Love Affair*. Like
the reviews of the first volume [*Year of Grace*], it is very favorable;
"the book captures the heart of prayer, etc." That is pretty funny
because both You and I know how distracted my prayers are and
how terribly imperfect these reflections are.
   Beats me.
   If there's any good in it that affects people's lives, it's Your
doing. And I'm grateful.
   Maybe I can learn from our conversations these days a little
more about focusing and witnessing and delineating myself from
You as You lurk within me.
   I hope so.
   Help me.
   I love You.

July 12, 1992 — Grand Beach

My Love,
   Two hours ago there was a report on radio that the pope
would have surgery tomorrow (or perhaps tonight). A stomach
infection or something of the sort, perhaps related to the wound
when he was shot. That news stirs up all kinds of ambivalences
in me. First of all, as a fellow human and as a Catholic who
respects the bishop of Rome I pray for his health. Secondly, as
someone who studies papal elections I found myself looking up
flight times to Rome — who knows what will happen? Thirdly,
as a sociologist who studies the condition of American Catholics — and indeed someone who is currently analyzing (vacation
or not) the catastrophic collapse of the Catholic sexual ethic — I
can't help but wonder what this crisis may mean for the church.
As a sacramental institution we depend on and are more com-

mitted to human leadership than any other Christian church. We have been especially troubled in the last twenty-five years by the breakdown of communication between the leadership and the rest of us. As a result, the enthusiasm and the positive energies unleashed by the Council have turned destructive. The next papal election will take place when it is Your will, but it will be very important. Very, very important.

JP II is a tragic figure — a man of enormous talent and ability who has misread the situation. Even his theology, as Gerry O'Collins reviewed it in the *Tablet* last week, is extraordinary. But his cultural perspective has led to the decline of the credibility of the Vatican to both Catholics and those who are not Catholic.

I surely agree with his opposition to the confusion of the last quarter century and to his disgust with some of the craziness. But it is not merely the crazies who have been punished or whose wisdom has been ignored.

Such wonderful opportunities have been wasted.

What comes next? Can we still have a new era before this century, this millennium, is over? I hope and pray so, but I leave that to Your wisdom and Your time.

And I keep my one eye on the airline schedules.

I love You.

July 14, 1992 — Grand Beach

There are so many things to worry about!

And, of course, there is nothing to worry about.

I finished this morning Lord Bullock's book *Hitler and Stalin*, a historical masterpiece, an object lesson in evil, and an overwhelming description of incredible human suffering. If You suffer with us — and I believe that You do — how much You must have suffered through those terrible years between 1939 and 1945, the years in which I was growing up. Now, almost a half century later, the war is finally over, though hardly in Bosnia (for whose people I pray), and the great pall placed by those two men on Europe is lifted or at least lifting. Europe survived, though just barely.

How strange and unfathomable are Your ways.

Yet You loved with an enormous passion each one of those persons who died during the terrible years.

I do not know what to make of all of this on this gray and gloomy morning. Today all I can say to You is that.

And that I love You.

July 15, 1992 — Grand Beach

My Love,

Ah, the sun is out and the sky is clear and I was able to go to the beach for the first time in days — and water-ski too! What a change the sun makes in my life. No matter how discouraging the world around me, an afternoon like this one gives me an enormous lift. I feel *good* again. Thank You for making days like this and especially just now this day!

The pope was operated on today. Pretty clearly he has cancer, despite the lies the Vatican tells. And bad at that. How could they let that happen! There are tests, easily done and painless, for exploring colon cancer. Obviously they did not use them. Will they ever get over the pope worship, which is ultimately so harmful to the person of the pope? In any case, and despite the murmurings in one part of my self, I pray that he recovers and that he suffers little pain.

The pedophile stories are now filling the newspapers. I think we've won the war on that one. I thank You for having alerted me to the problem and inclining me to fight it. I am glad I'm on the right side in it, though I surely won't get credit from my fellow priests. I hope that the solutions are not too painful for the church. I also hope that the Northbrook case is cleaned up soon so that justice is done there and the cardinal, poor man, can put that problem behind him.

He's off to London today for a vacation. I hope he relaxes. Take care of him too, as well as the pope.

I love You.

July 16, 1992 — Grand Beach

My Love,

I'd like to reflect with You during the next two days on Terence Fretheim's book *The Suffering of God.*

To begin with I am impressed by the portrait of You which emerges from the Hebrew Bible. The "God of Wrath" image, which was once so popular with Catholic teachers, clearly does not even begin to do justice to You or the Bible. You are, on the contrary, a very "human" God. As Fretheim says, Israel did not know an unincarnate God. You were depicted as showing Yourself in vulnerable human form. My friend (and Yours too) the Rabbi is right: In Israel there is a *demand* for Incarnation.

Often this "humanity of God" is dismissed as anthropomorphism or a sign of early stages of religious development but, as Fretheim says, the imagery runs from the earliest to the latest of the sources in the Hebrew Bible. Moreover, the point is rather that humans are theomorphic, created like God. Once one understands that all talk about You is metaphorical then the issue becomes how much a metaphor tells us about You. I must say that the metaphors of the Hebrew writers give a much more vivid and appealing image of You then do the metaphors of theologians today, especially those who do not want to offend modern "secularists" by suggesting (heaven save us) that You are a "personal" God.

When one ponders the metaphors, one (this one anyway) concludes that You are a pretty nice person — involved, sensitive, compassionate, sympathetic, tender, determined. What kind of a God would You be, I ask, if You were not of that sort? Indeed, as I was reading the book yesterday, I thought I knew You better than I ever had before.

And liked You better!

I hope in these reflections in the next several days to learn more about You and to love You better.

July 18, 1992 — Grand Beach

My Love,

Surely one of the most powerful and poignant themes in the Hebrew Bible is that You suffer *because* of us. Indeed in such books as Isaiah, Jeremiah, Ezekiel, and Hosea, the prophets present You as brokenhearted because You have been rejected by Your beloved people. As I reflect on Fretheim's book and the mass of quotes which establish this theme, I am amazed at how completely we have ignored these themes or dismissed them as mere poetry and subject to critique by the categories of Greek philosophy and theology. You tell us through the prophets that You suffer because we don't respond to Your love; then the theologians dismiss this and say, no, God can't suffer.

The prophets are, of course, talking about their experience of You. They are using metaphors to tell what they think You're like. But if we reject these metaphors we reject the experience of You that is the basis of our whole tradition. If we say that a brokenhearted God is theologically impossible (as my friend Hans Küng does), then we threw out the whole tradition. We have to say, I think, that Your heart is repeatedly broken, though not in exactly the same way as human hearts are broken. But don't we have to add, "even more than human hearts"?

Even as I write these words I find them hard to believe because they run so against not only the theology but even the catechism I learned as a boy. You suffer *because* of me? Well, yes, but, I am inclined to say, not really. If I mean that then I am rejecting as unacceptable one of the major themes of the Hebrew Bible.

Not right.

You expected so much of Your people. You expect so much of Your children — like any parent. You expect so much of Your beloved, like any lover. And how often You have been let down, not to say betrayed.

I am sorry.

I do love You and I will try harder.

July 19, 1992 — Grand Beach

My Love,

I'm feeling old these days. Maybe it's the three weeks of non-summer weather. Maybe it's the enthusiasm of little kids on the beach. Maybe it's the movies about older people I've been watching for my brief report to be released in August. Maybe it's the report itself. Maybe it's the weariness of too much exercise. Maybe it's the novel I wrote last month. Maybe it's reading books about the thirties and forties. Maybe it's discouragement over a lot of different things. Most likely it is that I am indeed old and have just begun to notice it.

My body grows weaker, my energy dims, my awareness of my own mortality increases, my health (still good, thank You) is less perfect. I don't have all that much time left. I've done a fair amount with my life, but just now on this chilly Sunday morning it all seems like a wasted effort.

I had a terrible dream early this morning about being back in Quigley [the junior seminary] and being subject to all the pressures of clerical culture against which I have raged recently. I don't like being an outcast from the presbyterate. I never wanted to be that. But I sure as hell don't want to be part of that culture again either. I suppose that reaction is part of my sense of being old.

I don't feel old when I'm not tired or discouraged. But I am old and getting older. I should be joyous about an exciting life and all the hints which surround me about Your love. But I'm not. Not today anyway, and I'm sorry about that. Help me please.

Back to Fretheim tomorrow.

I love You very much.

July 20, 1992 — Grand Beach

Another gloomy morning — three weeks of such mornings. I feel rotten. But enough of that and to the more important question about whether You feel rotten. The data from the Scripture say that You do. You suffer, something like the way we suffer and yet different from the way we suffer, as Fretheim says; once You decided to create, You put limitations on Yourself to be intimate with that creation and to love the creation, especially creatures that are in Your image and likeness. The promises You have made to us (Promise, maybe) is a self-imposed limitation, however Greek philosophy and theology may try to duck that truth. There's no doubt that the Hebrew prophets experienced You as Someone who suffered with and for and because of us. How terrible it has been through the Christian centuries that we have essentially denied that truth. More suffering in that for You?

How does Your suffering differ from ours? I'd guess that in Your case there is no fear of death involved in suffering and in our case there is. You are not subject to death (though Jesus was, Your ultimate gift) and You know that we, Your beloved children, will eventually not be subject to it either. There are other differences too, I'm sure. But the metaphor still holds, something like human suffering happens in You, something very different too, but something for which human suffering is an apt metaphor.

I remember back in the early years of grammar school we were told that our sins hurt You. Then we learned later on that You could not be hurt. Now I find myself back to those primary years and understand that You can be hurt and are hurt and that I have hurt You.

All I can do, all any lover can do, is say that I'm sorry, except now when I say it, there is perhaps a little more sense that I have caused pain in You and that the pain is real and like human pain, if also different from it.

I am so very sorry. I'll try not to do it again and I'll try to make up for it by being more generous and loving.

Help me to be that.

July 21, 1992 — Grand Beach

My Love,

Fretheim's second theme is that in the Hebrew Bible You suffer *with* us, You weep with our weeping, You moan with our groaning, You sorrow with our sorrow. Again our Greek metaphysics tries to explain all such metaphors away. But to do that denies the prophet's experience of You, an experience which surely is a prelude of the Incarnation. A God who does not suffers with us is not the God of Israel.

Most of the pericopes are about Your suffering when the people are invaded and oppressed and destroyed by enemy armies. Even in the prophets the image of You relating to a people rather than to individual persons is dominant. But there is no reason why that image cannot be extended to include everyone as persons.

Thus You suffered with Your people and with everyone else who died during World War II, the most horrible war in history (in which sixty million died). You suffered with each individual death, the way a parent suffers with the death of a child, but even more so. You suffer with the people who are dying in Sarajevo, with the guard who was shot at the courthouse in Chicago yesterday, with the innocents killed in northern Ireland and in Englewood in drive-by shootings (Englewood making Bosnia and Ulster look peaceful by comparison), and with the families who are left behind in all these deaths.

That's a heap of suffering.

It helps people who mourn to hear that You mourn with them. For so long we have foolishly not said that. How repressing was our theology.

And how generous You are to take on such a tremendous amount of pain.

Eventually, and I firmly believe this, You will wipe away all our tears and we will be happy again, young again, laugh again.

Like little children playing on the beach.

I love You.

July 23, 1992 — Grand Beach

My Love,

I seem to have a migraine headache. If Fretheim is right — no, if the Hebrew prophets are right — and You suffer with Your people, then You suffer with my headache. I hate to think of You hurting with such a trivial thing as my aching noggin, but that's the way mothers and fathers act, isn't it? If only we could have taught that through the years we'd be a in a lot better position with our lay people than we are now — and they would have come to know and love You better.

There is another pedophile scandal shaping up in Chicago. This time a lay employee of the archdiocese molesting children here from Ulster on a summer program. Am I to believe that You suffer with all of these sufferings?

Of course I am to believe that!

And also You suffer *for* us! There are certainly hints of that in the Hebrew Scriptures, and of course it is confirmed through Jesus. Just as human parents suffer so much in raising their children, so do You suffer for us as we struggle to achieve spiritual maturity. How great Your love for us! Help me to grasp this important truth and to return Your love!

July 24, 1992 — Grand Beach

My Love,

Yet another gloomy day. July has been a waste as far as sun and rest, and now more guests start to come. I'm afraid I've blown it. It will be hard to get back to these reflections but I'll try. I'll also try to be a good host, because my guests represent You.

July 28, 1992 — Grand Beach

The last of the guests goes home today and I don't have any till next week — when the cardinal comes! It was a good weekend, lots of fun, but not much time to relax or reflect. How many times have You heard me say that before!

Will there ever be time to rest? I feel so old.

If I am to believe Fretheim's wonderful book, then You feel the way I do because You are my parent and You suffer with me. That's a dazzling, indeed overwhelming thought, so big, so staggering, so (to use a word I don't like) ineffable that I can't comprehend it, especially when I'm so earth-bound, body-bound as I am this morning.

Anyway I do believe it and when I get back on course as this day wears on, I'll try to absorb it a little more.

Why is my spiritual life always about getting back on course? Why does every new onslaught of effort and responsibility, even pleasant effort and rewarding responsibility, sweep me away from the Spirit?

Because I'm human, I guess.

I'm sorry that I'm always beginning again after a lifetime of trying but also grateful for the grace You give me to begin again. Help me today, my dear love, to lift my heart and my mind and my spirit and see You smiling in the sunshine (which we now have had for two days!). A sacrament of love!

July 29, 1992 — Grand Beach

My Love,

I read Susan Howatch's latest book (*Mystical Paths*, as if You didn't know!) yesterday. A strange mix of Charles Williams and Anthony Trollope, but alive with Christian and indeed (Anglo-) Catholic faith. More than any of her other books it deals explicitly with good and evil, light and darkness. Ms. Howatch lives in a world thick with grace and dense with psychic powers which are not always grace and sometimes can work against grace, but which also can be grace. She has so much more vivid a sense of the presence of grace in the world than I do, and of the presence of evil too, though both of us see much of the evil as well as much of the grace coming from family life, and both of us have our wise priest—Lewis Hall in this story and Blackie Ryan or Packie Keenan or Lar McAuliffe in mine.

Writing about grace is tricky because grace is tricky, because You are tricky! In my stories it is usually cross-gender grace, kindled by passion and pointing towards freedom. In her stories grace for her men (women don't matter that much in her books, though I'm sure she'd disagree) usually comes from other men and almost never from her women. If I'm to judge by my mail, the readers understand the grace theme, though perhaps I should try some variants on it.

I come away from her book with a vivid sense of her own faith, faith in You, faith in the church, faith in Jesus, faith in resurrection, and — here she and I do the same thing — faith in the second chances.

I do believe that. I also know it to be true from the experiences of life. One must be willing to start over again.

Each day.

Like today.

I love You.

July 30, 1992 — Grand Beach

My Love,

I read Stephen King's new book yesterday. You play a part in the story, and the heroine keeps her promises to You once she escapes. As usual King ends the story with a "little bit of hope," all that is needed to keep us humans going.

Hope is the ultimate sacrament, the last love sign that is left when all else fails. We can't help hoping (even on crummy days!) because it is programmed into us to hope, even when the situation is most hopeless. And the ultimate question is whether such hope is a genetic trick played on us by a cruel and arbitrary evolutionary process or whether it is faint rumor of angels, a whispered message from You.

And even if it is a trick, how come "evolution" is smart enough to play that kind of trick?

There is certainly a lot of ugliness and evil in Your world. King's book is about a woman who was abused by her father. I also glanced at a book about Bruce Ritter last night. More evil. The corruption of the innocent all around us. If You suffer with us, and my reflections this last week tell me that You do, how much You must suffer at the abuse of little children!

All will be well eventually, that I firmly believe. But eventually is a long time in coming. In the short run there is so much horror. I must do what I can to stop some of it, which is not very much.

And the church looks so bad, so embarrassingly bad. That's not new either, but the failure to deal adequately, even today, with the pedophile problem is tragic.

Gloomy thoughts for a gloomy day, but I love You and always will.

July 31, 1992 — Grand Beach

My Love,

July goes out with an autumn storm. Whoever said global warming! As You know, I'm a little worried about the new novel. For sheer story it's my best ever. It has wonderful characters, and the religious message is strong too. I hope it will be successful.

I admit to You that my fear of failure is deadly. Or rather that I fear a failure which would be deadly. I never expected to write bestsellers in the first place, but now that I have written them, I fear falling off the lists. It is a ridiculous fear. There are still hundreds of thousand of people who are dedicated fans and I need have no financial worries, though perhaps I would have to stop funding some of the people I've been funding. After the focus session this morning I may be less fearful, but I will still be anxious in the next couple of weeks. And I will continue to pray to You that this book catches fire, as the fire on the cover suggests that it should.

At the heart of it all is my fear of the Great Depression, which has been with me all my life — small wonder given the terror it was in my childhood. The sense of the bottom falling out is indeed terrifying. But if I trust You and Your love for me I know that everything will eventually be all right. All manner of things will be well.

I love You. Help me to have confidence in Your love.

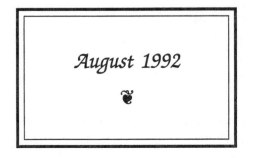

August 1992

August 1, 1992 — Grand Beach

My Love,

The poems I've been reading these last couple of mornings are about heaven, the world-to-come, whatever. They seem kind of archaic to me in that they take the clouds and harps and angels approach — there is not enough continuity between this world and the next. The conviction has grown with me through the years that there is an essential continuity between the new earth and the new heaven. But the question of what is to come once again raises the question of who You are.

I certainly picture You as a far more intimate friend than do the metaphor makers I have encountered the last day or two. I acknowledge the "majesty thing," as our incumbent president might say, but I can't pray very well to majesty; I can to an intimate lover, a metaphor I would not dare use unless You had revealed it to us.

Do You really exist at all, much less as the kind of God who wants to be an intimate lover?

Finally there is no conclusive proof, only hints, sacraments of love all around us — like the visit from an old friend yesterday at noon and the rich blue of the sky when the clouds cleared away this morning and the music of Haydn which softly plays as I do this reflection. How can one reject hints, "come-ons" like these?

I can't and that's why I love You.

August 2, 1992 — Grand Beach

My Love,

Yesterday was lovely and so is today, and I'm obviously re-laxed because I am forgetting things as I usually do when I'm relaxed. It's only taken six weeks, but that's all right! Thank You for finally pushing me into a state of relaxation. I hope my wan-derings on the book promotion tour next week don't destroy it all.

Also grant that the book is a success. Please.

The other night I watched *Experiment Perilous*, a 1944 movie with George Brent and Hedy Lamarr. It was the first time I'd seen Ms. Lamarr in a film. She was the Marilyn Monroe of her day. I think I stayed away because her first film *Ecstasy* was given a "C" rating [condemned] by the Legion of Decency (fleeting nu-dity which, I gather, would be mild by today's standards, maybe PG–13!) and we were warned to stay away from films in which she appeared. I believe she is still alive, married to a German in-dustrialist and millionaire, and has collected all the old copies of *Ecstasy* that she could and destroyed them.

She was not, it turns out, a "sexy" person at all, in the sense of the various current "bombshells," but she was an extraordinar-ily beautiful young woman, pale, fragile, frightened rather than erotic, but nonetheless breathtaking.

She is still alive, and surely much of her very youthful beauty has faded. I have no idea what she is like as a person and of course one ultimately must respond to a real woman as op-posed to a screen image as a total person. Yet such beauty, which inevitably fades with time even if the total person becomes more attractive, is a hint of Your beauty, a sacrament of Your attractiveness, a rumor of the glory of the angels. A love sign.

It is tragic that beauty must fade into the corruption of the tomb. But as someone who believes in You, I also know that somehow it will be restored, and that You and all the beauty which reflects Your Beauty will conquer death and corruption. If life is too important ever to be anything but life, so is beauty too stunning ever to be anything but beauty.

This I do believe with all my heart and soul and hence love You very much.

August 3, 1992 — Grand Beach

My Love,

I want to begin today by praying for all those affected by the recession, which now seems to be worse than anyone had thought. I wish especially to pray for the various members of my family who got hit by it last week. Help all who have been hurt by these hard times and help our country to pull out of it.

There was a curious contrast on TV Friday afternoon. First, the five o'clock local news reported stories about the priest from Kankakee who was arrested for child abuse (after leaving some pictures of such behavior on videotape, which he then sold as a second-hand tape!).

Then on the 5:30 ABC World News Tonight, the "Person of the Week" was a Jesuit who had made peace among Hispanic street gangs in the poorest parish in LA. One end of the priesthood to the other! I'm trying to persuade the cardinal to do a column on the subject.

Far more priests are like the Jesuit than are like the man from Kankakee, but the latter, along with a few ex-priests with chips on their shoulders, are shaping the image of the priesthood. To make it worse, when a good priest is written up (as Pat Lee was in the *Wall Street Journal*) too many other priests turn against him, not realizing that when one priest is celebrated, the whole priesthood is enhanced! But we can't leave those positive stories to chance.

Anyway, it seems to me that if the priesthood is in trouble, it has only itself to blame. While priests on the average are happier than married men of the same education and income (as Tom Nestor's sociological work shows), they cover this up by letting the unhappy and the perverse shape the image and then complain about the attention that some good priests get who might enhance the image.

So next week I go off on a promotion tour, which I hope will also contribute to the image of the priesthood. I will get no acknowledgment for that from many of my fellow priests, but that ought not to matter. I must only be fully aware of who I am and what I represent when I balance my various roles in such interviews.

Help me to do it right. Help the book to succeed. Help all of Your priests, flawed humans that we are, to make it through the present crisis.

August 5, 1992 — Grand Beach

My Love,

Well, today is the day of the dinner here that the cardinal is going to cook for the mayor and Maggie, a gourmet northern Italian dinner!

Sometimes I wonder why I get myself into such goofy experiments. I have two friendships, both old, one recently renewed, and while they're not exactly at stake, it won't be comfortable for anyone if the dinner freezes up or if nothing happens, much less if something unanticipated goes wrong.

My agenda is modest, a good and relaxed time for everyone. The possibility of a fruitful dialogue. But that may not happen automatically. However, I can't cause it to happen, so I'll make my best possible contribution by being laid back and relaxed, my most leprechaunish self.

Anyway, please bless this madcap adventure and help it to produce a good outcome for both the city and the archdiocese.

I love You.

August 6, 1992 — Grand Beach

My Love,

The results of the dinner were about what I had expected. Good food — indeed excellent food — a pleasant time, but not much dialogue. Maybe if we could have lingered longer over the drinks more would have been accomplished. It was at best a good beginning.

The veal scallopini was terrific.

I love You.

August 8, 1992 — Grand Beach

My Love,

Four more weeks of summer, two of them marred by having to leave Grand Beach. I am depressed by that thought and I ought not to be. Quite the contrary, I should be grateful for the blessings of summer, and for all the blessings of my life.

Having said all that, I am still depressed.

Maybe because I dread next week and its travel and rush. Just now I'd really like to retire — quit the sociology, quit the fiction, quit everything but weekend Mass. Just now most of what I do has lost its savor.

That won't last, or at least it has not lasted before. It's a phase which has happened many times, but again just now all the fun has gone out of life. I am so tired of rushing to catch up, of trying to remember everything. So tired.

Help me to snap out of this interlude and to recapture my taste for my life and work.

I love You, even if today it doesn't sound much like it.

August 9, 1992 — Grand Beach

My Love,

What an incredibly beautiful day yesterday was! As Sean Durkin noted, it was too wavy to ski on Lake Michigan and there was not enough wind to sail, but apart from that it was heartbreakingly lovely — cruisers, sail boats, wave runners, floats, kids, teenagers, parents, grandparents, absolutely clear blue sky — all the glory of summer time on a mighty lake.

And as I told folks at Mass, it is all a reflection of Your glory. Either yesterday was a sacrament of You or nothing makes any sense. It would be hard on a day like yesterday to avoid the former conclusion. So I thank You for the glory of the day and promise my love to You.

And, You'll note, I refrain from complaining that I will be away from Grand Beach during the best week of the summer.

Grant that the book does well. I love You.

August 11, 1992 — Chicago

My Love,

Yesterday was a hard day, and today and tomorrow will be even harder. I had no idea that novel writing would impose such problems on life.

Being a successful novelist, something I never expected or indeed sought, is not all that it is cracked up to be. On the other hand, I'm glad and grateful that it happened to me, no matter how much the strain might be. I hope You don't mind if I say I'd rather be at Grand Beach.

I ask You to grant that everything goes well. Take care of me on this trip.

I love You and I want to love You more.

August 17, 1992 — Grand Beach

My Love,

Life is crowded. And I'm dry and dusty spiritually because there has been no time to do anything but run. I'll try to make up for it in the next two days. I feel so much like a spiritual infant, but You still love me no matter how dry I am.

Do I seem a disappointing lover to You just now? I have been preaching single-mindedness for the last several Sundays, and I'm not very single-minded myself. On the contrary I am spread out all over creation. So many projects, so many worries, so many responsibilities. Mary has chosen the better part, as Your Son says in the gospel, but I have not been able to choose that part as much as I would like or would want or should.

The promotion last week went well enough, though on this morning as I come up for air, I wonder if it will help the book all that much. I pray that it does.

I'll be back tomorrow and a little less exhausted than I am today.

I love You. Help me to be more dedicated in that love.

August 18, 1992 — Grand Beach

My Love,

Reviews and stories are beginning to appear. *Newsweek* yesterday, the *Tribune* and *Commonweal* today. The first was fine, the second okay, the third terrible, a typical but no less heartbreaking assassination. The *Commonweal* article says that *I* say that I'm doing something right in my fiction because of the sales and the money I make — *an outright lie!*

That goes with the territory, I guess. I shouldn't let it upset me. Yet it is like someone has vomited all over me.

I should not reply and I guess I will not reply — unless June [book publicist] tells me to, and I'm sure she won't.

The boat broke down again today before I was able to ski.

What can I tell You! And I'm still dry as dust!

I love You. I'm sorry for my present discouragement and depression. I know You didn't intend me to travel.

I'll try tomorrow.

August 19, 1992 — Grand Beach

My Love,

Lots of dreams last night about violent combat, doubtless a reaction to my anger over the *Commonweal* attack and all the other problems of yesterday. Why do I get so bothered by such outrageous lies? I must get ready for my guest today and the guests over the weekend (help me to serve You by making them comfortable), prepare for the trip to the American Sociological Society tomorrow, get the boat fixed and respond to some of the attacks — all on a day that was designed to be a precious breath of relaxation.

I am, as Hopkins says, "sand shift in an hour glass, as stable as water in a well."

I'm sorry, truly I am. All of my worries and concerns and responsibilities are not worth the energy they consume, the peace they shatter, the distraction from You and Your love.

I am such a child spiritually.

I am so sorry. Help me to love You more and better.

August 20, 1992 — Grand Beach

My Love,

What kind of a man is it, I wonder, who saves a clip from *Publisher's Weekly* from 1987 to use against me in an article and then lies about what the article says? I ponder this question as I reflect on the attack in *Commonweal*. Did he deliberately lie or, more likely, is his mind so twisted and sick that he saw in a text that had nothing to do with my books and contained nothing like the words he attributes to me what he says in the text?

It is not pleasant to know that there are people out there who are that twisted on the subject of me, snide, sneaky, passive-aggressive, sick people who vomit their self-hatred onto me. It is not reassuring to know that I have become an inkblot for sickies. I've know this for some time, of course, but this example was particularly egregious. I pray with the psalmist that I may be protected from such people. They are dangerous because they would kill if they could. And a magazine like *Commonweal* which will print such lies!

I know You love me and I know that I will be eventually protected from such people. But memories of my stolen files and all the lies and the hatred at that time resurfaced this week. It's kind of scary to know that such hatred lurks out there and that it will strike whenever it can without warning and indeed without mercy.

With Your grace I survive and I pray that I may continue to survive against such folk. Please protect me under the shadow of Your wings. And don't let me lose my inner serenity (such as it may be!) because of these attacks.

I love You.

August 22, 1992 — Grand Beach

My Love,

The panel at the American Sociological Association went very well thank You. But I confess that I thought as I came back in the plane last night that I am a little tired of being so many different people. It is easy enough to move from one of my roles to another, but they all take increasing amounts of time. Admittedly I don't have a family and that gives me more time than most people but nonetheless one of the reasons I feel harassed is that I have tried to do too many things. Moreover, I've added a few new responsibilities each year.

I know that I've gone through this with You before to no avail. But time and age does take its toll. Ought I to cut back and if I do, what?

Sociology? Fiction? Parish work? Columns? Teaching?

So it doesn't look like I'm any closer to a solution than I have ever been. I just want to say that I'm tired and discouraged because there is so much to do and because the year that starts in two weeks looks so crowded.

Anyway, I thank You for the success of the session in Pittsburgh, and I love You and want to love You more.

August 24, 1992 — Grand Beach

My Love,

I had a wild night of dreams last night — will there ever be a night of peaceful and restful sleep again? This time the dreams were about parishes, as they so often are. I was much younger and was given a chance to be a pastor and continue my work of writing and research. Naturally I took it! I suppose the dreams were a lament for the loss of the archdiocese and perhaps for youth too, for a time when there were more opportunities and options, a lament for the end of summer and the end of life.

Pretty grim stuff, wasn't it!

But the galley proofs of my book of poems that Ashland Poetry Press will publish this Fall came in the mail today and gave me a nice surprise. I had to read eighty of them together and was pleased to see how light and hopeful and lyrical they are. Another side of me. Two visions of my life very much at odds with one another — laughter and hope and lyricism on the one hand and weariness, discouragement, and grimness on the other. Which is true, which is valid, which better expresses my present condition?

I guess I can't choose, but I am tired just now, and I do feel old, and I do wonder about the purpose of all my work and effort and concern and responsibility.

And I have to go to the dentist this morning, which is always a grim affair.

I sound like I feel sorry for myself, don't I? Enough.

Protect all those in Miami and environs as the hurricane sweeps through today.

I love You. I don't want to sound like I'm complaining.

August 26, 1992 — Grand Beach

My Love,

It would appear that the big pedophile story might appear in the *Trib* after all. I have mixed emotions about this. First of all and most important, it will at last give the persecuted families a clear voice in the Chicago media of the sort to which they have long since been entitled. It may also finally move the church off dead center in this case and perhaps the civil authority too — though both have resisted unfavorable publicity before. On the other hand, it will hurt the priesthood and the church and the cardinal. In particular it will weaken the impact of the reform mechanisms the cardinal has instituted.

You well know how hard I have labored in the last nine months to prevent this from happening, and I'm sad that the institutional culture and the denial mechanisms have prevented it. If the article appears as written, it will invite the whirlwind. Grant that this case and the whole problem will be cleared away in the near future.

I love You. Help me to love You more.

August 27, 1992 — Grand Beach

My Love,

I'm reading Anthony Trollope's last novel, ironically called *An Old Man's Love*. Trollope was sixty-seven when he wrote it and was in great physical discomfort from his various ailments. He would be dead within the year. Yet, as the introduction says, he wrote with much of his old vigor and wit. Moreover his books were no longer as popular as they had been and he didn't need the money, so the only reason for writing was love of story-telling — a love so great that he had to dictate much of the story because writer's cramp from his twenty-five hundred words in the morning before breakfast had ruined his writing hand. It's a fairly melancholy story with the self-destructive heroine who seems to have been typical of his final stories.

All of this is interesting to say the least for someone like me, who is only three years younger and whose books are widely read but not as popular as they once were. I don't have to write, but I do love storytelling, although I dread the responsibility of starting to write a story — as I dread the rat race when I return to Chicago.

But I have good health (for which many thanks) and my stories are still about You.

I will be dead soon, even if the soon is twenty years, which I guess is about what my life expectancy is. I will stop writing soon, though I'm not sure when that will be. What do I have to show for my life of hard work, controversy, and weariness? Not much, but something, I guess, and maybe that's enough.

It is a particularly gloomy day with the rain about to start and last all day long and myself with guests coming. So much going on, so much conflict, so much weariness — and this the end of a vacation! Tomorrow perhaps I turn to poetry. That might help.

Despite the gloom I cling to my love for You.

August 28, 1992 — Grand Beach

My Love,

Priests for guests yesterday, lots of talk, great dinner party, mayor in fine form. I'm terribly tired this morning, no energy at all. Sleepy camper. Desk loaded with mail. Another job of copy editing to respond to. Excuse me please but the sensible thing is for me to go back to sleep, which I am doing immediately.

August 29, 1992 — Grand Beach

My Love,

What am I supposed to do? What should give in my life? What responsibilities should be ignored? What activities curtailed?

And how many times have I raised this question with You? Yet nothing changes in my life.

Sometimes the very people who tell me that I should say no to many things, that I'm too generous with my time, are the first to impose new responsibilities.

I am unable to say no strongly enough and really mean it. That would be a great grace.

This really can't keep on the way it has.

Help me, as the psalmist this morning is so confident that You will help him.

August 31, 1992 — Grand Beach

In the Axial Age, according to John Hick, there was a burst of optimism. Humans began to believe in the need of salvation/ liberation. It was possible to break out of the routine, usually sad, of everyday life and death. The emerging world religions thought that humans could escape from the cycle of life and death, which the nature religions tried to balance. I would call his "optimism" *hope* and believe that I am an heir of that extraordinary human breakthrough.

It provides something on which I must mediate as I experience the end of summer, today being the last day of August, the failure of my new book to make the bestseller list, the nearness of death, weariness with the pace of my life, and the tremendous amount of work which faces me in the year about to start. I should add my utter lack of motivation to return to work. I have never been so reluctant to settle down to the demands of September.

All of this is precisely the cycle of daily life from which the axial religions promise salvation/liberation, though in the long run at best. I do believe in the triumph of spirit and person, in freedom and union, in all the good things that You promise. I do believe with Julian of Norwich that "all things will be well" and that "all manner of things will be well." I do embrace the hope which was unleashed in the first millennium before the common era. Somehow, my Love, these beliefs don't energize me this morning. I had thought of starting my mystery story today, but it is quite impossible. I'll put it off till the day after Labor Day, however much that may complicate the rest of the year. There's no point in rushing, is there?

So in theory and in faith I subscribe to hope. In practice I'm still mired in the end of summer. Okay, maybe it is good to stay mired here for awhile.

I love You.

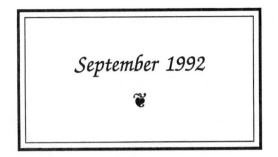

September 1992

September 1, 1992 — Grand Beach

My Love,

An aspect of John Hick's book which disappoints me is his rather easy acceptance of what I would think is a weak pluralism: All the world religions say the same thing, and the differences in their content are the result of cultural conditioning; one accepts this even if it makes one a bit uneasy when singing the hymns of one's own tradition.

David Tracy and Hans Küng are much more rigorous. One holds to one's own tradition and is open to listening and learning from others. Hick's relativism strikes me as being typical of many liberal theologians — so eager to understand and praise the other that they forget what is unique and special about their own. You don't find the other making that mistake often.

Here is where I really part with much of the fashionable self-hatred in the West. Not all cultures are equally beneficial, and not all world religions are equally valid. As a Catholic I must be open and ready to listen and learn from others, but that does not mean that I think my encounter with You in my heritage is not special and is indeed not the best.

I do not think that in any other tradition, not even those of the Book, I would dare to speak to You with the intimacy that I boldly claim in these reflections. For that privilege I am very grateful. I will not say that it is no better, in this respect at any rate, than any of the other traditions. I am grateful for it and I love You.

September 3, 1992 — Grand Beach

My Love,

A bad night because of more pedophile trouble in the archdiocese. I should do nothing serious after supper at night.

And dear [Bishop] Clete O'Donnell is dead. May You have already granted him permanent happiness. He was a good and wonderful and fascinating man, who was dealt a good hand in life up till the coming of Cardinal Cody and a bad hand after that. He should have been a major archbishop and an important voice in the American church. We would not have had many of the problems we currently have if that had happened. Instead he was frozen out because of his integrity and intelligence. His own melancholy Celtic temperament, made worse by diabetes, tormented the last years of his life. You never promised a rose garden to any of us or said it would be easy. Living is hard; dying is hard. I've been lucky in my life so far. There is no reason to think that the luck will continue. Help me to live well in whatever crises remain ahead of me even if and when things go badly as they almost certainly will.

I trust You and I love You and I believe that the best is yet to come.

September 4, 1992 — Grand Beach

My Love,

First guests are here. So the busy weekend begins. But while I still have a chance I wanted to reflect a little while I still have a chance. Hick makes an interesting observation about belief in life after death. He says that humankind in the Preaxial Age may have engaged in wish fulfillment, but as far as we could go was sheol or hades, which were pretty bad places, shadow lands much inferior to this world. Only in the proto-personalism (my phrase) of the Axial Age did the world religions conclude to full survival, union with the Ideal in Plato, resurrection for the Pharisees etc. We became aware of the possibility of a grand survival only after we began to get hints of what You are like. You're not wish fulfillment, whatever else You may be, You are the result of our experience of You, an experience which it took a long time to recognize.

Why did Your self-disclosure take so long? That's a good question. I'll have to ask some of my theologian friends about it. However, I do live in the Postaxial age, and I am blessed by a deeper knowledge of You and greater hopes for what You have in store for me.

I presume in ages yet to come, our species will learn even more about You, especially as it reflects on Your self-revelation in Jesus (and Jesus-like others, though none are quite like him). I hope so.

I don't know You very well, but I am grateful that I know You as well as I do. Help me to know You better and love You more.

September 5, 1992 — Grand Beach

My Love,

I talked to the cardinal last night and felt compassion for him. He's rushed as always (makes my life look easy) and unaware of just now much trouble closes in on him. The pedophile mess does not improve despite all his efforts. There are so many angry people out there. The VOCAL meeting will bring them all together, and an outburst of anger will be directed at him. He would be so much better off if he resolved the Northbrook matter before then. But he's locked into a "will-to-believe" on that.

This next week should be hellish for him with both a national TV program and a two-article series in the *Trib*.

Thank You for the friends and family in the house and for the possibility of this weekend. I love You.

September 7, 1992, Labor Day — Grand Beach

My Love,

Yet another nice day, a perfect Labor Day weekend, for which many thanks. We went to Saugatuck on Friday, a nice trip. When we came back I dug out an old picture of my mother visiting there (probably crossing the lake on a liner, one of which is still in the port). She was a young woman then, quite pretty and self-confident. My own memories are not of that woman because they are blurred by the woman with Alzheimer's, the widow who lost her husband when she was still in her early fifties, and the woman whose life was shattered by the Great Depression. Poor kid, I think looking at the picture, she had a hard life, not as bad perhaps as did her own parents or relatives in Ireland, but still a hard life, so hard and so disappointing that I could not imagine it.

And I have a summer home in Michigan and fame and I travel the world. But it does not follow that I am any happier or that my life has been any better or anything else, except maybe that I've been luckier.

I thank You for all the blessings, and I'm sorry for all my failures. I love You.

September 8, 1992 — Grand Beach

My Love,

Summer and vacation are over and it's time to get back to work on my sociology and my story and also shed some of the excess weight of the summer. I thank You for all the graces of the summer, for all the recreation and the good times, for the books read and the friends entertained, for the sun and the sky and the lake.

I turn to my work again with something of a sense of relief. I look forward to these next three weeks with only one interruption as a time of rededication in a relatively peaceful environment, for which I am also grateful. October and November will be very busy so the more productive work I can get out of the way up here the better. I intend to finish a couple of articles and reviews and write most of my new Blackie story. Then I can do the reader in sociology during the next three months and prepare my lectures in Tucson for the spring quarter. During that quarter I'll work on my new autobiography volume. Then a year from now I'll probably have enough data for the big sociology book.

An ambitious but not impossible schedule. Help me not to push too hard.

I love You — You who are summer all year round.

September 9, 1992 — Grand Beach

My Love,

I've been reading chapters from Joe Blotner's life of Robert Penn Warren, a brilliantly written and compelling story. He quotes at the beginning of one chapter the following lines from one of Warren's poems: "We live in time so little time / And we learn all so painfully / That we may spare this hour's term / to practice for eternity."

Warren is presumably talking about an hour of lovemaking with his passionate if eventually demented first wife. But his insight applies to all our hours. He felt that the "death" of orgasm was a hint of the nothingness of real death — since he had no religious faith. But he could have as well said that the ecstasy of lovemaking was a hint of *You.*

We do have so little time and we do learn so painfully. By the time we have some wisdom (and at best that's precious little) our life is mostly spent. Each hour given us, particularly after the end comes near and with it some sort of wisdom, is practice for what comes after. So the hours I spend these weeks in trying to tell a story are in their own way practice for eternity, work indeed but also an attempt to illumine Your love, a privilege, a joy, a blessing. Help me to act that way through three weeks and to love You more and better as I am more conscious of working in Your service. Help me also to have confidence in the power of Your love.

I reread the lines from "Red" Warren. I wonder how ecstasy could not have been a sacrament for him. I'm sure You loved him too and took care of him.

So many mysteries in life.

September 10, 1992 — Grand Beach

My Love,

In my readings for today, I encounter men finding safe havens: Hopkins's poem "Heaven/Haven," a psalm in which David takes refuge in the temple, and Ed Selner's diary bringing him to Maynooth where he is treated with warm Irish hospitality.

They are all seeking protection, Ed perhaps less than the other two, David from those who would kill him, and Hopkins, if I am not imagining too much, from his Jesuit superiors and colleagues who would have destroyed him and his work. I wonder why those who do great or even good things stir up such enmity. I have never been able to understand the resentment against me. It astonished me when it first surfaced and, while now I know all the reasons for it, it still astonishes me. I do understand, however, the need for a haven like this place where I can in a certain sense escape from it all. At last I'm now turning off the phone in the morning and with considerable success — though it still bothers my parish priest conscience just a little.

So much of the tragedy of human life comes from irrational hatred. Why do men and women bother with it? They must hate others, I guess, because deep down they hate themselves. Yet they make the world an unpleasant and sometimes dangerous place. I know that many of those who hate me know nothing about me or my work but merely project their own problems onto me. And others approach my work with a determination to twist it so that it fits their own preconceptions.

I can't curse them like David does. In fact, I have to feel compassion for them and pray for them that they break out of the bonds of hatred. Yet I also am glad of the bastions of protection and safety I have and I beg You as does the psalmist that You protect me under the shadow of Your wings.

And that You help me from being too disturbed by them.

How is it that obsessions with hurting other people can become the fundamental concern of a human life?

So please continue to protect me in a very dangerous world. And keep me in Your love.

September 11, 1992 — Grand Beach

My Love,

As You well know I'm in the midst of a novel, a Blackie Ryan mystery. In it I try to wrestle with issues of good and evil, of love and hatred, of the divine and the human. I hope that there is hope in the story, the eternal possibility of redemption. I think my confidence in my storytelling is declining, both because they are no longer big bestsellers and because of the criticism. The criticism does have an impact on me; it creates doubts and uncertainties which depress me. The work continues, I write what I can, but I don't value what I write, at least not enough. Somehow those many hundreds of individual readers who write the nice letters don't seem to counteract the nastiness of the critics, not as far as my morale goes anyway. Of course many people would be so devastated that they might never write again. I have thick enough skin so that I keep writing but not enough self-respect to dismiss them as extraneous to the readers who care. Well, I am what I am and what You made me but I wish I would value the positive reactions and ignore the negative ones. Why do I let them deprive me of my happiness?

I love You. Help me to understand that You love me.

September 12, 1992 — Grand Beach

My Love,

Tomorrow's *Trib* (available this afternoon) will allegedly have the definitive Northbrook pedophile story. It has been a long time coming. The Chicago media have ducked this story for years. I have mixed feelings about the story because, on the one hand, I think an account of how the church continues to oppress its own people even while it is sincerely trying to work out a new approach has to be told if one expects the oppression to stop. I have worked for a couple of years to see this story told because justice demands that it be told.

On the other hand, I have also worked since my reconciliation with the cardinal to get this case settled before the firestorm began. I made a little bit of progress, but it came to nothing. The cardinal has been ill-served by his lawyers in the past, some worse than others. Moreover the church is caught in a mammoth institutional denial mechanism which prevents it from seeing the truth. The church will probably circle the wagons and hunker down after this week of terrible publicity.

I had relatively little to do directly with this article. I talked to the mother once about it and that only briefly. Indirectly, of course I am responsible because I have been on this subject for seven years. In either case I will be blamed. That doesn't make all that much difference.

I wonder what will happen now after the firestorm. At first nothing, I suppose. Then maybe as time goes on the church will realize that it is caught in the wrong strategy. But the harm that will have been done to the priesthood and the church will be terrible. And much worse the harm done to the victims, about which the church still doesn't even seem to care.

Grant that it may not be too late for something to be worked out to bring this horrible case to an end.

September 13, 1992 — Grand Beach

My Love,

I'm now in the throes of the new novel. It is coming along and it is fun to write though it consumes everything in life. And during the Notre Dame–Michigan tie yesterday, my mind was more on the story than on the game. It is a great gift, as someone told me yesterday, to be able to write stories the way I do. It is indeed, as I realize not for the first time, and for it I'm very grateful and for the blessings which flow from it. I find it hard still to value and respect that gift enough.

A call from old friends the day before yesterday. I've known them since the days of their courtship. Wonderful couple. They have had a tough life recently, family and health problems which would break most marriages, but somehow they have managed to cling together. Now, even though they are old and infirm (as much as I hate to say that) they seem to love each other as much as ever.

Two conclusions: One, life is a vale of tears; many of the hopes with which we start out can be cruelly destroyed. Two, love still survives.

I don't know what to make of it all, except to feel with these people and admire their courage. And to tell myself that You love them and have through the years and that You will wipe away every tear and increase their love. What else can be said?

I love You.

September 14, 1992 — Grand Beach

My Love,

The article in the *Trib* yesterday was a model of restrained and responsible reporting. My own private poll, neither large nor random, showed that the laity responded with horror to what the church has apparently done in this case — that is, they believe the *Trib* story and they believe the parents. We'll see what the second half looks like today. The church has only itself to blame for the story. I have no regrets that it appeared, only that the church has acted so badly.

Will it never end?

The writer who is preparing the article on me and my bête noir has suggested to me that it is a powerful love/hate relationship on his part, most likely founded on some latent and perhaps unrecognized homosexuality in him. It sounded crazy at first, but I must say it fits the data and is probably true. I felt sorry for him. The article, should it ever appear, will devastate him. Again I regret that, but I don't regret that the record is set straight. There's no way one can get into a relationship like that.

I would have never thought that I was the kind of person who could be the target of such emotions. It boggles my mind that I am. How do you avoid them? You don't, I guess.

An odd world we live in and an odd species we are part of. I pray for him and for the cardinal. Help them both. Help me to be more realistic and alert.

September 15, 1992 — Grand Beach

My Love,

There was an act of terrible cruelty reported on TV last night, just a brief story from Washington. Two car hijackers stopped a car at gunpoint, threw a woman and a baby out of it, and drove off at high speed. The baby's mother was caught in her seat belt, dragged for two miles, and killed. Teenagers. Nice kids. Destroyed a family. Surely some folks will use the poverty of the killers as an excuse. I wonder if we will ever progress beyond violence in this country unless we stop making excuses for crim-

inals. But my reflection this morning is not so much about crime
and criminals as about the random violence of the world. Abi-
mael Guzmán, the would-be Mao of Peru, was finally captured
yesterday. For more than a decade he and a small band of fa-
natics have killed over twenty-five thousand people in Peru as
he tried to create a Communist state by terror. Another Stalin,
another Hitler. And there are American liberals who seemed to
approve of him.

Our lives are so fragile. We live on the edge. Random violence
can destroy all our dreams. This morning our world looks like
a terrible place. I know that You take care of us and love us all
as Your children and that all will be well eventually. I know that
death finally does not triumph. Yet in the interim it still seems
ugly and terrible.

I watched Kuroswa's film *Dreams* again last night. Such
beauty and such ugliness. And for all my faith in You and all
my experience in life the mystery of the combination of the two
of them still overwhelms me.

Well, I must get on with my novel, perhaps to finish today,
certainly tomorrow. I hope I am a little successful in my efforts to
tell the world of Your love.

And I do love You.

September 16, 1992 — Grand Beach

Couldn't sleep last night so I'm up at five o'clock. Too much
yesterday. Work on the novel, phones, doorbell, general harass-
ment, dumb interviews, doing two or three things at the same
time. So I'm up to work on the novel. Maybe I'll be able to go
back to sleep. Too much discouragement. Terrible, terrible day.
What is all of this about? What is this crazy month of October
that's coming up all about?

I don't know.

The novel comes well. I like it. It's fun. But I am so discouraged about everything else.

I love You.

September 17, 1992 — Grand Beach

My Love,

Today is the forty-fifth anniversary of my father's death. I was reading through some of the family archive material which Mary Jule [sister] has prepared and came across her account of him. Though she was in eighth grade when he died, she has a remarkably accurate portrait of a remarkable man. My own images are clouded over by time and memories of the impact of the Great Depression on him. I remember the silent discouragement and the integrity and the hard work and the great respect others had for him. I have a hard time getting back to the real man, the energy and the wit, the determination and the charm, the ambition and the intelligence. Maybe I will get to know him better in the world-to-come.

By virtually all worldly standards I have surpassed him. You know well that I set out seeking none of these things but only to live up to the ideals he set. I suppose I've been doing that all my life and my outputs in various fields are all an attempt to live up to that ideal. Is that good or bad? A mixture of both, I suppose. Good because I strive to do good and be good as he was, and especially to be fair. Bad because I am driven more than most people and more, as You well know, than is compatible with a prayerful and reflective life. Yet on balance, I think, as long as I am aware of the dynamics it is not altogether bad to want to show this man that I want to be as good as he was, though, despite all my achievements, I still have the feeling that I'll never be that good.

I have said often that all I ever wanted to be was a parish priest. Was that really true? Given the drive and the ambition, would I have ever been content with that? I was certainly happy in that role and am still happy (happier?) when I play that role. But I probably needed something more. Well, I've found the something more and it is beyond my dreams or plans. You provided the outlets for my energies and for that I'm grateful.

Anyway, thank You for the inspiration that my father provided. And the warmth which must have been there for me to be what I am even though my memories of the warmth are blurred by the tragedy of his later life. I'm sure You've granted him peace and happiness long since, but because I believe in prayers, even retroactive prayers, I pray for that too.

And I love You.

September 18, 1992 — Grand Beach

My Love,

A dark, dark morning with rain pouring down, kind of neat. Autumn. Life goes on and so do the seasons and that's hopeful too. I'm going into Chicago today for the opening night of the opera. I'll also see the cardinal about his new rules for pedophilia. He seemed better last night when I talked with him. The crisis goes on.

My spiritual reading is about loneliness today, and Andrew Marvel celebrates solitude in the poem I read. Two sides of the same coin. Marvel even says he prefers solitude to a wife, and that the unmarried man who is alone is twice blessed.

WELL, as one of my teenage characters might say, I'm not so sure about that. I do appreciate solitude, not that I experience all that much of it. Up here with the phone off people still ring the doorbell and flood me with fax messages as they did yesterday. Real peace and solitude is hard to come by in this world. Maybe I'd like it if I could find it. But real loneliness is hard to experience, though I guess lots of people experience it not because they are alone but because they feel cut off from everyone — as close to hell, I should think, as we can know on earth.

I've never really experienced either solitude or loneliness. Too busy for either, I guess, even when I travel alone, which is no substitute for traveling with others. When mixed with jet lag, it can make one feel odd, to say the least.

But hardly lonely.

Well, what can I say? I thank You for protecting me from loneliness. I thank You for blessing me with friends and a communication network. I accept the lack of solitude which comes with it,

If I really want solitude — and I just might next week — I can always pull the plug on the fax and put a do not disturb sign on the door, can I not?

And write poetry, which would be a nice end-of-summer activity.

I love You.

September 20, 1992 — Grand Beach

My Love,

When I went into Chicago on Friday, I turned off the air conditioner. When I came back today I turned on the heat for a few minutes. Thus does summer turn into autumn as the equinox approaches. In any event, thank You for the season.

Also thank You for Rossini's "Othello" last night. A lovely work. So much beauty as well as so much hate in Your world. I thought how dumb poor Othello was to be taken in by an envious go-between. But I've been taken in by such folks too, I guess.

I saw Eamonn Casey yesterday. He seems resilient. A man of enormous energy and enormous faith. Take good care of him. No matter what happened, he has served You well.

I also saw the cardinal this morning. He and John O'Malley showed me the rules for the new review board regarding sexual abuse. It looks good. The board itself looks good too — five out of the nine members are women. I don't think the clergy will like that, but it's high time. Unfortunately he is still trapped in the bad legal strategy on Northbrook; one of his lawyers is supposed to have said that two male egos stand in the way of the settlement of the first suit, the cardinal's and the lawyer's. My guess is that it is the latter more than the former. But the new procedures and people are promising. Twenty priests have been removed from parishes — how incredible that would have been just a year ago.

I feel compassion for them too. Help them and protect them. And the cardinal and the church.

Such a terrible mess. But so much is.

I have but a week left here, with basically not much to do except to write a little poetry. Help me to take advantage of these precious few days.

I love You.

September 21, 1992 — Grand Beach

My Love,

The equinox, the end of summer, the beginning of autumn, my last week here. I celebrate the coming and going of the seasons and all the blessings of each season. I thank You for the stars and the moon and the sun and the rain and the wind and the waves, and all that makes the world in which I live lovely and varied and exciting and interesting. The psalmist this morning sees the heavens as reflecting Your glory. It is easy for us, knowing what we do about the cosmos, to think that it is no longer true and to lose our sense of awe and wonder when in fact what we know is even *more* marvelous and staggering than what he knew.

How little attention I pay to such things. The other night I looked and saw perchance the moon. I marveled at its glow and then went back to whatever was occupying me. What a waste of a gift! Help me (I ask knowing how vain is the prayer), to be more aware of Your beauties all around me, as I would the beauties of a lover. I say "vain" not because of Your lack of generosity, but because of my own deeply ingrained habits of work. Perhaps the poems of this week will help me to change just a little. I pray that it might be so.

And I love You.

September 22, 1992 — Grand Beach

My Love,

It's two in the morning and I'm not able to sleep, too much work and tension yesterday — and no poetry despite my great intentions in the morning. Foolishly I tried to work on charts and watch the Bears game at the same time. I ought to know better. Today (when I wake up) I'm definitely going to write the sonnet which has been crashing around inside my head. I already have the first two lines, "The other night I looked up and saw the moon / near my kitchen window lurking in the trees / it was bright and silver full," and so on. But I should have done it today and I'd be sleeping now.

The psalmist today pictures himself surround by enemies in time of war and places his trust in God and not in human power. Presumably David also had a pretty good army. But still he was right. Armies aren't enough. They can't protect you from death or death's thousand hints. How much of my frantic effort and work is really an attempt to do it all myself without relying on You. I know You love me and will take care of me and that I should worry about nothing, but how many projects I juggle in part at least because I do want to do it all myself since I don't trust You completely. I ought to know better. I really should. I'm sorry. I think now I'm tired enough to go to sleep. I love You.

September 23, 1992 — Grand Beach

My Love,
   Yesterday I watched (while I was finishing up a redo of my charts on prayer!) a video documentary about the "weeping Madonna" at St. John by God in Chicago, or so it was called by many of the parishioners. It was a first-rate flick. It would have been so easy to satirize the people and their faith. But the filmmaker was rigorously objective. Only at the end, when one of the nuns cursed the cardinal and hoped that the "Blessed Mother" would blind him, did the anger and superstition which lurked behind the devotion emerge.
   I must say that the film stirred up all kinds of complex emotions in me. The pastor who presided over the devotion and was eventually banished is a classmate of mine. He doesn't seem to have changed much, either physically or psychologically. Moreover as a proponent of the popular tradition, I have always acknowledged that it can go awry. But I guess I had forgotten how far awry it often does go and how important the high tradition is as a corrective.
   Moreover, often the high tradition has only itself to blame for troubles like the St. John by God affair because it does not offer much for the faith of the simple folk like those elderly people who were left behind when the parish folded. Particularly in the years after the Council it has written off so much that was good and useful and harmless instead of rearticulating it. My sympa-

thy went out to the poor people of St. John by God. The high church had failed them and the popular church misled them.

The balance is a delicate one but essential. I must make this point clear in my presentations.

As You know, I yield to no one in my admiration for the Mother of Jesus, indeed I imagine You as being much like her. I am angry at the corruption of what she stands for by such a "cult of the marvelous." But I am also angry at those who think that she is a disposable image and not the privileged image of the Catholic tradition.

I must keep this clear in my own mind as well as in my public comments.

Help me to understand how easily we misunderstand the nature of Your love.

And help me to love You more and more.

September 24, 1992 — Grand Beach

Autumn Moon

I looked out the window late last night
And saw there the moon, lurking in the trees,
How rich and full she was and silver bright
She wanted only to pose for me and be

A sacrament of woman, love, and God
Beguiling me with her misty, magic light.
Yet I turned away — how terribly odd —
And, oh, pushed my naked moon out of sight.
So little time ... I could not permit her tease —
She tried to ravish me, poor thing, but lost the fight.
For my precious work I must each minute seize;
Thus I rejected her and, ah! destroyed delight.

Moon and God, I love you both, but on my knees
I plead: not now, come back some other night!

Help me never to turn my back on the moon — or You.

September 25, 1992 — Grand Beach

My Love,
  Another poem to offer to You:

> I was afraid when I was a little boy
> A storm like this might herald the world's demise,
> The day of wrath which will end hope and joy
> As sun and moon vanish from the skies.
> The clouds are dark and mean and low,
> The air is thick with portent and dread,
> The angel might any second blow
> His trumpet to wake the living and the dead.
>
> The apocalypse is now long delayed
> And only in wild metaphor described.
> Yet of this autumn storm I'm still afraid
> And tremble at the thought of God defied;
> For someday soon my fragile life will end
> Pie Jesu, dona mihi requiem

Indeed, grant me Your peace.

September 26, 1992 — Grand Beach

My Love,
  Last day at Grand Beach. Rainy and cool, end of summer. I am so sorry to see summer end and I so dread the schedule which faces me for the rest of the year. Nonetheless I thank You for the summer. I do feel much better than I did at the beginning and I look forward to the excitement if not the rest of my return to Chicago.
  I am so fortunate to have a place like Grand Beach to which I can come each year and revel in whatever a given summer has to offer. Again I thank You; I can't believe how fortunate I have been. Again I'm sorry; I can't believe how stupid I've been in not making the most of Your blessing. Take care of me and protect me in the months ahead. I love You. Help me to grow in my love for You in the busy days and weeks and months to come.

September 28, 1992 — Chicago

My Love,

The city is so beautiful! I'd like to look out the window and praise You, but I've had two phone calls since I began this reflection. So it will be and so it will go. I'm already tired. I find myself thinking that retirement might not be a bad idea, if only to protect me from the fax and the phone and the media and airplane trips. But they'd probably go on at exactly the same rate.

I will try once more to keep You in mind as I rush through life. I realize that on the basis of my past performance there is ample reason to doubt that I can do it, but I hope to try. I love You and I want to show You my love in everything I do and say.

There goes the fax.

I'll bring the computer with me on the trip and try to reflect with You each morning. Help me to relax as best I can.

I love You.

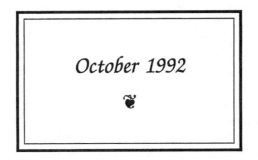

October 1992

October 2, 1992 — Washington, D.C.

My Love,
I reflect today on the discomfort and inconvenience of boarding an airplane at National Airport. Not hell certainly, but for a poor traveler like me, surely something like purgatory. There seems to be a law against getting a plane loaded here efficiently and getting it off on time. I will be so glad to get home.

The Catholic TV programs I taped were not all that exciting, though some of the people were pretty clearly afraid of me, for reasons that have more to do with their preconception than with any propensity of mine to eat interviewers alive.

Supper at the Wallaces' was fun last night. A Clinton pollster was there and reported that the entrance of Perot into the race was not likely to affect the outcome. He compared the unease of the Democrats to that of the Eastern Germans when it looked like the Berlin wall was about to come down. They couldn't believe it would really happen. Nor can Democrats believe that the long era of Republican folly is coming to an end.

I long so to be home and unhassled. I love You.

October 5, 1992 — Chicago

My Love,
Life is back in order again, I have a couple of weeks without any travel, time in the morning for spiritual reading, and an op-

portunity to reflect in some kind of peace at the beginning of the day. It's always been easier to be a spiritual person when my life is orderly — which suggests how weak my spirituality is.

Anyway I am now reading Ralph Harper on "presence" and find it very exciting. Despite all the skepticism and pessimism in the world, he says, we all have repeated experiences of "presence." He uses the small "p" advisedly because he is speaking of many difference kinds of presence. All of which, I presume, suggest Presence, but I'll have to wait till I get further into the book to see if he gets to You — the Presence behind the presences. I presume he will because he is a cleric, indeed an Anglican priest. A Catholic priest, I suspect, could not be quite as reflective as he is, not today at any rate.

I also read about pilgrimages, journeys in a direction — a voyage filled with presence as well as Your Presence. I wish I didn't tire so easily. Then I could comprehend both the journeys and the presences better than I do. But You made me the way I am and weariness is part of the game for me.

I am still weary this morning, even though life is beginning to fall into place again.

I love You.

October 6, 1992 — Chicago

My Love,

Harper writes today about our intuition of presence, a subliminal preconscious apprehension of You (or Being, if one would rather use that code), as propounded by such varied thinkers as Eckhart, Heidegger, Levelle, and Rahner. We are too busy, they all say each in their own way, with beings to be aware of our contact with Being.

And they are dead right. One has to be a dedicated skeptic to be unaware of presence. Wonder won't go away, as in my tardy wonder of the Indian summer glory of our city these days. Where there is so much to wonder about, there must be something full of Wonder. Wonderful!

Last night, after I was awakened by an obscene phone call (wrong number, I think), I read the current issue of *Discover* about the ten great unsolved mysteries of the universe — how old it is, order and chaos, whence life, are we alone, etc. Impressive puzzles. I thought about the men and women who probe these mysteries. Do they wonder? Are they aware that they are in touch with Being? Do they understand the marvelous mysteries which surge all around them. Perhaps some of them do. And perhaps many are like me — impressed by Being but too busy with beings — work, family, students, career — to be able to pay much attention to the Wonderful.

That's what You are, You know, Wonderful.

And I think like James Joyce You delight in puzzles and mysteries. That too is wonderful.

I love You, wonderful You!

October 7, 1992 — Chicago

My Love,

Two wonderful thoughts from Harper: "The mind is a traveler waiting for the train to paradise to start." I'd say turn the train into a 747; but the point is the same. And, in an allusion to Bernanos: "The secret of life is not the pursuit of happiness, but the discovery of joy."

In both these lovely comments I encounter the truth that joy is present and so is paradise, sometimes, even when you don't want to accept the ultimate basis of that joy and that paradise. It's still there — the taste of the madeleine at tea, a church steeple, Indian summer sky. Joy recalled, joy rediscovered, joy with us even now. Again in Harper's words: "You open the closet door and there is Narnia — past, present, and yet to come."

Despite the phone.

Yet the phone (which has interrupted this reflection five times in the past twenty-five minutes) makes it tough.

Help me to become more aware of Your presence and the joy of that presence.

October 9, 1992 — Chicago

My Love,

Harper talks about the loneliness of the dark today and how it is in a certain sense a "refraction" of the light, of presence. You become aware of presence when it is refracted by its absence. He cites the case of the frightened and lonely Proust lying in bed in his hotel room in Balbec, seeing the light under the door and rejoicing at the coming of morning, when it is only the corridor light and it is still midnight. The memory of that moment of absence in itself refracts presence.

As You know I was once afraid of the dark, and now revel in it, as my Dublin poems from last year reveal. I believe You are there in the dark, lurking, waiting, loving (as did John of the Cross). I now love the dark as much as I once feared it. I don't like gray days at all, indeed days like this one depress me. But real dark, not as a negation of light but as a sacrament itself, I love. Not as a refraction of light but rather as a time of mystery and wonder and awe, an interlude filled with presence. I must write more poetry about that. And I must finish my barely begun Indian summer — oops, Native American summer — poem. For which I am sorry.

I know about presence; I experience it. But somehow there is no time for it in my life.

Help me to give myself more time and more freedom to come to know You and Your abiding presence more completely and more fully.

I do love You very much.

October 10, 1992 — Chicago

My Love,

A talk out at Marist High School for "Jesus Day" this morning, lunch with Larry McNamara, class reunion on the morrow — more busy times, but good times.

I think again of the quote from Bernanos — life is not the pursuit of happiness but the discovery of joy. If you don't have it, then no way you can get it. How true, how powerfully, pathetically, perfectly true!

Help me during the events of the next two days to be as aware as I can of the presence and the Presence around me and, insofar as I can, to reflect that presence in word and deed and in my own presence. This despite the cold or the sinus or whatever which is hassling me.

Oh, please, help me to be more aware of the real presences which surround all my life and for which I am deeply grateful, even if I don't show it all that often.

I love them and You.

October 11, 1992 — Chicago

My Love,

"Reality has deceived me," thus does Harper quote Proust in my reading today.

"The only real paradises are paradises lost."

"Life is an express train ride which does not stop at the expected stations."

Wow!

Harper argues that for Proust there was presence which he would not or could not admit, just as for Heidegger there were presences he knew but could not quite describe.

Maybe Proust's sexual orientation was the reason he thought that he had been deceived, an understandable reaction perhaps, especially in his time and place. It is easy, however, for anyone to think that reality has deceived them. I wonder how many of my grammar school classmates with whom I will meet in a couple of hours would feel that reality has deceived them. Or have felt that way — perhaps not in so many words — at least some of the time.

By and large, reality has not deceived me, though I think the priesthood, as a cultural collectivity, and the church, as institutional authority, have both deceived me. Or at least revealed to me my naiveté. But reality has been good to me, better than most. There have been times when it has not seemed good, but those moments have been infrequent. There will be bad times doubtless in the years to come.

But it is not good or bad times about which Harper is talking. Rather it is a sense of the goodness of life, the goodness of existence, the presence of being, to use his words. Despite the fact that my sense of Your presence is often weak and distracted, I do, because of Your grace, comprehend it, experience it, believe in it. For that I am very grateful. Help me to maintain that sense in the days and months and years ahead, however long or short they may be.

And help me to be a sacrament of Your presence at the reunion this afternoon.

Let them see that I do love You.

October 12, 1992 — Chicago

My Love,

I wonder why the reunion yesterday was such a magical, graced event. Perhaps because for a couple of hours we were all young again, perhaps because we encountered old friends, perhaps because we remembered more vividly the good times together and forgot the bad ones (well, my accursed long memory didn't forget everything, but that's another matter). We all wanted to preserve the event, keep the minutes from passing by, see each other next week. None of that will happen, but it was the way we felt as we remembered together the way we were.

I do believe that some day we will be together again, we will all be young again.

I guess You heard my prayer about my being a sacrament. Many people said that I seemed such a happy person because I was smiling all the time. In fact I had a terrible nervous headache through much of the day. But, as I explained to the people I drove home, I smiled and talked to everyone, worked the crowd like I was Rich Daley, because that's what priests do or are supposed to do. "How much you've changed," they said. Have I really? Perhaps. Perhaps not.

Am I the happy, smiling priest they claimed they saw? I hope so, sometimes at least, because of Your grace. Many said they thought they knew me well because I came into their homes on TV so often. Here is another group to whom I feel responsible and for whom I must be careful to be the kind of priest I should be.

Anyway it was a wondrous event. I'm sorry it had to end. Thank You.

Also, if You can arrange to get through to the dunderheads in Rome and make Larry archbishop of Omaha or Kansas City that would be a great good work for the church.

I love You. Help me to keep alive the wonders of yesterday.

October 13, 1992 — Chicago

My Love,

Class reunions, I now think, are only partially nostalgic recollections; they are more fundamentally and primarily exercises in hope, even if the hope is subliminal and unperceived. We encounter men and women we have not seen for a long time, maybe as long as fifty years.

They have changed, heaven knows, but they are still the same in many ways. The continuity with the past suggests that there is something in each of our reencountered classmates which transcends time. If we can be young again, however temporarily, at a reunion, maybe it is possible to be young again — young but experienced — in some transcendental fashion. That which survives in the persons and the memories may somehow be imperishable. The reunion is a rumor of angels and the joy that comes from that rumor is the hint that what we were and what we are is, just perhaps, what we will always be.

Larry made that point very neatly in his wonderful stories. You love us because You see in us the fair spouse. You ignore our imperfections and You revel in our goodness. You, who are responsible for all of us, were there at the reunion, having as much fun as we all were and know for sure as we did not that it was more of an anticipation than a remembrance!

It was several hours of the presence about which Harper writes!

You were there with us! How wonderful!

I love You.

October 14, 1992 — Chicago

My Love,

I didn't sleep too well last night, partly because I watched the silly vice presidential debate, but mostly because I spent the day reading, which is normally quite relaxing. However, the books were the ones I bought on Monday at the university: All the history and the violence and the color of Alexander the Great, violence and sacrifice, eighteenth-century English marriage customs, and mysticism in the early modern era made my head spin vivid and colorful and crazy images. Most of all I was impressed and depressed by all the human suffering in the books (except, perhaps, the last one). The men and women whom Alexander killed, the victims of human sacrifice, the abused men and women of the old system of marriage. I wanted to pray for all of them, to ease their pain, to wipe out their heartache. What a cruel, evil species we so often are!

I knows You feel the same way about wiping away the tears of each single victim, far more than I do. Any God who would not would not be a God worth anything — a *deus otiosus*. Nor would any God who didn't care about them be the God who You claim to be.

I don't understand it all, it's the greatest mystery of all — well, no, the second greatest. The first is why there is anything at all. The second is why, given that there are things at all, why there has to be so much suffering.

Anyway, the answer is always the same: I have to trust in Your love and Your ability in the end to wipe away every tear. You love each of us, more than we can possibly imagine, more than we love our most passionate other. This I do believe... and end as I always do with my weak attempt at a response: I love You.

October 17, 1992 — Chicago

My Love,

There was a grace yesterday for which I am very grateful. I had barely come into the apartment when Dan Weil called from

City Hall to say that Kathleen Turner wanted to meet me. She was here to be honored by the Chicago Film Festival. So I went to the ceremony and then to the reception afterwards (sponsored by Pieper Heisdeck champagne!) and was introduced to the actress (who is something else altogether, a powerful sacrament of You) and gave her a copy of the paperback edition of *An Occasion of Sin*. She said she had bought the hardback and had already read it *twice*. I said she'd make a good actress for the heroine and she said she'd be good at all my heroines, but the one she most wanted to be was Gabriella the seraph in *Angel Fire!*

As the kids say, like WOW!

I'm still floating around on the clouds!

It doesn't necessarily follow that anything will ever happen, and I'm not ecstatic about that so much as that her verdict is a tremendous vote of confidence — which I need just now.

So thank You for that vote of confidence. And for meeting another sacrament of Your grace.

I love You.

October 18, 1992 — Chicago

My Love,

Sunday morning. I must rush out to VOCAL. I hope it goes well.

Harper writes about presence invading through the senses, especially smell and hearing — two senses I pretty much ignore, the smell because my chronic sinus doesn't permit me to smell all that well (though that is probably a cop-out) and hearing because I am too busy with too many things to listen.

Since I read that passage, I've tried to be attentive to sound and smell with only meager success. It is so difficult to undo a lifetime of habits — and the racing of mind to the detriment of all else.

A city like Chicago is filled with sounds: the wail of fire engines and ambulances (which still wake me at night and scare me), the clang of traffic, the melodies of street music, the murmurs of people on the street, snatches of conversation in many different kinds of voices, the throbbing hum of urban life. Yet I rarely notice them or permit You to manifest Your presence and invade me through them. I'm going to make a big effort this week to be more open to sound, to train my ear to pick up sounds, to find metaphors to describe them.

And if I improve on smell in the process so much the better.

Help me this week to at least listen a little better.

I love You.

October 19, 1992 — Chicago

My Love,

Another grace yesterday, for which I am deeply thankful. Erika called to tell me that a woman sociologist named Kiki Alexander (daughter of the late psychoanalyst Franz Alexander) died of cancer last week; the last thing she was doing before she died was reading my latest novel, taking great consolation from its story in her last moments.

That is, if You don't mind my saying so, pretty strong stuff. Kathleen Turner on Friday represented life. This poor woman represented death. My novels made a beneficial impression on both of them, the former non-Catholic, the latter Catholic. That's gratifying. I've always wanted my stories to help people be aware of Your grace in life but never pictured them helping someone to die. It almost gives me the shivers.

Of course the novels are about life and death and rebirth. They're meant to have that effect, but that's a heartwarming example of what I've always hoped for from them, an incredible contrast to the image they so often have with so many people who have never read them.

I am, need I say, very grateful for these two graces, especially at a time when I need the encouragement. You've reminded me that I do not labor in vain.

Thank You again and I love You.

Grant rest to my fellow sociologist.

October 22, 1992 — Chicago

My Love,

As You know, I went to the hospital yesterday for a routine chest X-ray (I hope and pray that it was nothing more than routine). Hospital visits are always sobering and depressing experiences because they bring one so close to mortality. I don't like them. As I was registering at the radiology desk yesterday, the clerk was reading a report off her computer to an M.D. on the phone. It was a death warrant for some poor person with lung cancer. Be good to that person, I beg You.

So much agony and suffering in a hospital. I have to believe that You are suffering with all the sick and with those who love them and that somehow, some day the agony will be gone and all tears will be wiped away. "And all matter of things will be well."

I really must get out and take a long walk on this lovely Indian summer day.

How do I contrast Indian summer (well, American aboriginal summer) and Little Company of Mary's radiology department?

I guess I can't. Not today. They are both part of life and that's the way things are. Your love lurks behind both of them. My job is to recognize the presence of Your love and reflect it to others.

I do love You. Please strengthen my faith and love.

I love You.

October 23, 1992 — Chicago

My Love,

Harper talks today about "theophanies," about Your breaking through into the ordinary life of ordinary people. He compares the psalmist with Proust, noting how conscious of Your presence and mystery was the former and how the latter fought against even the ordinary manifestations of Your presence in trees on a hillside.

I wonder about theophanies, whether in fact they were what they seem to be in their description. That David (or whoever) was conscious of Your presence I don't doubt, but that his experiences were all that different from Proust's or mine I am not so sure. As a believer he could see more in them than could Proust, and as a poet (a real poet and not an amateur scribbler of verse like me) he could describe them more powerfully than I can and hence make them even more important for his own life.

This ugly city of mine (to lift a word from Jimmy Joyce) is as filled with theophanies as was the French countryside of Proust or the Palestine of the psalmist. Harper, I think, is wrong to think there were once more theophanies than there are now, once more mystics than there are now. You're out there lurking like You always have been. There may even be as many people who are sensitive to Your presence, Your mystery, as there have always been. They're not the ones who write the poetry or the stories. And those like me who do write poetry and stories are too swept away by demands and responsibilities to write the poetry or to fill the stories with imagery like they should be.

There was so much of You lurking on my tour of the city the other day. So many love signs. I knew You were there, dancing for me. Yet I paid so little attention. I must, perhaps this weekend, try to write some poems or at least some lines which record Your presence in the city.

I love You.

October 24, 1992 — Grand Beach

My Love,

I'm here to preach at Jim Davis's church and give a bull session for Bill Henkel over at Notre Dame tonight. I don't know why I get involved in things like this, except that I can't say no to requests by friends. That's fine and virtuous and all that, but it does crowd my life so there's no time for reflection. A nice bind: respond to one's friends or reflect? I don't know.

A week to the election and two weeks to my Ireland trip. Clinton now seems to be losing his lead as Perot, that nasty little fascist, erodes his support. Bush may well be reelected. What a disaster that would be!

And another week till my Ireland trip — with two airplane trips and lunch and supper every day till I leave. What a hectic month it has been since I went back to Chicago from here. And to what point? That's the question — cui bono?

Reading Harper about Your presence and being aware that indeed You are present from the hints I barely notice I wonder if it is possible to change my life and how I am to do that. I don't want to keep up like this. No way.

Help me to love You more.

October 25, 1992 — Grand Beach

My Love,

The question I posed yesterday was a stupid one. Of course the two "favors" I did yesterday for friends were more important than a day of quiet reflection. I need a couple of days up here on retreat, a long weekend maybe after I come back from Ireland. But responding to the requests of friendship is a prior claim. The way to do retreat is to block it out in the calendar beforehand and then preserve it as part of my regular schedule. And that I will do. I regret that I have slipped out of the habit.

The Native American summer days continue to be lovely. I can't remember ever being up here at just this time. It's breathtaking this year, another revelation of Your presence and a spectacular revelation at that. And at least yesterday I took time to revel in it.

This is the change of the year, Halloween, foliage, end of daylight saving time. Winter's darkness is upon us. But that is beautiful too, as I learned last year in Ireland. Help me to be sensitive to Your reflections during winter.

Now I will turn to my Native American summer poem, which I started last night. I love You.

October 26, 1992 — Chicago

My Love,

Harper makes the point in my reading this morning that memory of the past is no substitute for the present. You can't go to bed with a memory, Harper notes crisply.

"Fersure," as the kids would say — though what Harper does not seem to see is that the memory of things past can become a present reality with a promise for the future. They were not for Proust (save perhaps occasionally and transiently), but that does not mean that the recalled past cannot be a sacrament for future realities or Realities. You can't go to bed with a memory but you can go to bed with a sacrament.

The trick, I think, is to be aware of the sacramental which lurks everywhere in the present, both with its recollections, its present experiences, and its anticipations. So our class reunion a couple of weeks ago was a special kind of sacrament because it had all three kinds of presence.

Help me in my daily confusion to be sensitive to the sacramental which pursues me everywhere — by which You pursue me everywhere.

October 27, 1992 — Chicago

My Love,

This morning my subject for reading and reflection is fulfilled desires. Harper argues, using Proust again, that fulfilled desires are in a certain sense worse than unfulfilled ones. As long as a desire is unfulfilled, the possibility that its fulfillment may bring us happiness keeps us going. Once it is fulfilled and we still have hungers, we are disappointed. I think of priests who looked forward to ordination, to getting out of their first assignment, to leaving the priesthood and marrying, and still are not happy. They suffer not from unfulfilled desires but fulfilled ones. Marcel was able to win Gilberte, Mme. De Guermantes, and Albertine, and none of them claimed Proust's restless heart. Finally he sought fulfillment in the memory of the young Gilberte brought back to life by her daughter.

"Our hearts are restless until they rest in Thee."

I think of all my fulfilled desires — to be a priest, to study sociology, to be free from the constraints of the institutional church, to write fiction, to become part of the archdiocese and the university again, etc. etc.

My hungers are still there. I will not say that I do not find some satisfaction and happiness in these fulfilled desires. They're nice. I'd rather have them than not have them. Unlike Marcel I do not dismiss them. But they do not satisfy me — as I knew they wouldn't.

Only One will satisfy me, only one Love.

I ought not to deceive myself about that.

Help me today to see Your love lurking in the work I have to do and the people I have to meet.

I love You.

October 29, 1992 — Chicago

My Love,

"The world is charged with the grandeur of God," wrote poet Gerard Manley Hopkins.

Even on a gray, post-Native American summer day like this?

Why not? There is beauty in the gray too. It is soft and restful and peaceful and relaxing. I need some peace to escape the noise of the election campaigns of which even I now have grown weary. It is a mean, nasty campaign, which is to say that both Bush and Rich Williamson, far behind in the polls, have sunk to new depths of viciousness in the last few days. I try not to watch TV and just glance quickly each morning at the polls I trust. There has to be a better way to elect a leader of this country.

Anyway, Your grandeur is present everywhere, even for those who do not see it. As I talk to You this morning I look out on the city and marvel at it as a sign of Your grandeur. The street lights are just blinking off, the streets are filling with traffic, people are going to work, the taller buildings hide in haze and low clouds. The city looks kind of peaceful, though I know it is not.

I want to pray on this sleepy, peaceful morning for all those in the city, each in his or her own way filled with Your grandeur, who are worried about their jobs, their future, their marriages, their families, their health care, and I ask that the country does a better job of taking care of its people, especially its poor people.

I wish I could help them myself in ways better than I do. But I'm not You.

I love You.

October 31, 1992 — Chicago

A quick Halloween reflection because I could only get to this now. That's not true as You well know, but You also understand the circumstances. I'm off in a few minutes for St. Mary of the Woods for Mass and then to the opera. Busy, busy.

I'll try to do something in greater detail when I get back — reflect on all the religious material I read today in working on my reader.

The opera was wonderful. I'm so happy for Bill Bolcolm and Artis Kanik. They deserved a winner and a winner they got, a modern morality tale, more stark and more powerful than the Frank Norris article.

A lot to reflect on about greed and about the flaws in our very human nature.

Now October ends, a busy, hectic, and, to be truthful, also exciting month in an exciting city.

I love You.

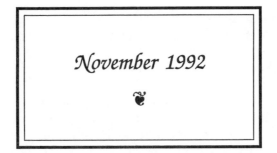

November 1, 1992 — Chicago

My Love,

I note that my computer clock still thinks it's Halloween when in fact it's All Saints'. Just goes to show you that computers are not perfect!

And a cold, windy, rainy All Saints' it is. November is here with a vengeance.

Again I rather like the rain and the grayness on a Sunday morning. But as You know it is in my nature not to like it very long. Every day in Ireland could be like this. Oh, well, the people make the country!

More about last night's opera, which seems even better this morning. It was a morality play about greed, as Von Stroheim saw when he made the film version back in the twenties, and more powerful in the opera, because more condensed than in the book. I've seen people turn that way, though perhaps not as thoroughly in their outward manifestations, just as the characters in the story of McTeague. So much of the resentment I encounter from many priests and ex-priests is based on the unspoken assumption that they have the right to the money they think I earn. Greed as well as envy. Both twist one beyond recognition, as Trina says in the opera, "What have I become!"

In that instant she wins salvation for herself, I think.

But I should be thinking not so much about my critics' greed, but about my own. I like the life I am able to live, the trip to

Ireland, the presents I can buy for people, comfortable seats on airplanes, state of the art computers, enough clout to get seats for the opening night yesterday. I do not think I am so attached to them that I could not give them up, though I would not like to have to give them up.

As always, one lives on the borderline between attachment and detachment. I would much rather write books that are read than make money from them. So my more serious vice could go in the direction of ambition instead of greed. But one must always be watchful, and the opera last night was a fitting bit of counterpoint to the feast of All Saints.

Greed and holiness are both options. To steer away from the former and towards the latter takes courage, self-awareness, and grace.

Thank You for the opera. Help me to continue to be aware of my dark side, to love You and grow in that love.

November 2, 1992 — Chicago

My Love,

Now it starts. Boston today and seven plane flights in the next eight days. Well, I feel pretty good — no, excellent — at the beginning of the ordeal. And [Dr.] Marty Phee reported that all was well yesterday. Thank You for the priceless blessing of good health and please continue to protect it. Also protect me on the various journeys I'll be making for the next three weeks.

I voted at 6:30 this morning for Clinton, who will surely win. Bless and protect him and his family too.

A fascinating quote from Harper this morning: "Nothing restores the sense of being alive less ambiguously than the rebirth that follows the appearance of the unexpected, the finding of a person that one did not know that one loved so much."

I've certainly had that experience in my life and am very grateful for it. I will reflect on it during my travels of the next two days. Help me reflect You during my travels.

I love You.

November 6, 1992 — Chicago

My Love,
Still rushing. Two weeks of running and then I'll be home from Ireland, hopefully with a week off at Thanksgiving.

Harper this morning alludes briefly to the Catholic doctrine of Real Presence and its decline in the post–Vatican II world with emphasis on meal rather than sacrifice and on community rather than presence. No more visits to the Blessed Sacrament, no more sense that Jesus is there in church.

I guess he's right. "Transubstantiation" is either in disuse or defined to mean something that it did not mean when we were growing up. Yet I think the doctrine is true and can be saved. You are present in every bit of bread and drop of wine as the Creator is present in the creature. You and Jesus are present in the Eucharist in a special way; it is a Real Presence though it may not be a physiological presence — one proven by stories about bleeding hosts. The faithful still believe that they are receiving Jesus and they believe rightly. It is the clergy and the theologians whose faith is weakened by a different explanation of the mode of presence, isn't it? We are paying the price for our excessive literalism of the immediate past. Real Presence will be rediscovered, especially because Presence is at the center of our sacramental religion, as my research indicates. The laity continue to be way ahead of us.

Help me to be always sensitive to Your Presence and Your love.

November 9, 1992 — Chicago

It is hard, my Love, to be aware of presence when you're tired. For all of Harper's talk about presence and all his accounts of Proust stumbling up against presence and not being quite able to cope with it, he does not take into account — nor does anyone — what it's like to come home on a Sunday morning after a weekend as a house guest, a perfectly delightful weekend indeed, but still one that in which you are under the stress of an unusual situation and an unusual bed anticipating yet another plane flight.

In moments like those one is truly at the mercy of one's crea-
turehood, quite incapable of even the slightest mystical feeling.
Then I read MacEwan's wonderful novel *Black Dogs* and came up
against the mystery of the presence of evil and the presence of
good — terrible evil and overwhelming good — both presented
by an author who tries to be neutral in the argument between
rationality and presence but in fact leans in the direction of presence. I note it with interest but I am too drained by my travels
this last week even to cope with it, even to cope with the most
graceful part of all, the narrator's admission that his mother-in-
law's experience of presence has made possible the happiness in
his life.

All too much but all very wonderful, in the sense of full of
wonder and what I should be trying ever more to do in my own
stories.

I'll be back on that story tomorrow and through the trip to
Ireland.

November 10, 1992 — Chicago

My Love,

As usual I don't want to make the trip which begins tonight
and I even ask myself why I'm doing it. The year is crowded
enough and confused enough as it is without my adding any
more confusion to it. Will this be my last European trip? If You
grant me continued life, probably not. Right now, however, I wish
I didn't have to go. But so what else is new? The trip will be interesting and exciting and exhausting. Help me to be patient and
gentle through it all.

One of the points MacEwan explicitly intends to make in *Black
Dogs* is that all suffering is individual and personal, not statis-
tical. Forty million deaths during the Second World War were
forty million personal moments of terror and tragedy — and all
the deaths since then. What a terrible half century — no, what a
terrible century for Europe and the world and how fortunate we
Americans were to escape most of it.

Is there any reason to look forward to an improvement in the
next century? Well, there have been no "world wars" for almost

fifty years and totalitarian tyranny is receding, but ethnic conflicts rage on. Maybe things are getting a little better. I hope and pray so.

What can I do about all the suffering and death? Not much, I guess, except be concerned about it and try to feel with it and write about it, all of which are pretty weak. A young woman over at Ann Arbor talked about her shock when she charged into the inner city as a doctor, prepared to save people and the world, and discovered that her efforts were mostly puny and ineffective.

The secret is not to quit. To keep trying. Just now I feel so tired and so little like trying. As I've been saying, it's hard to be aware of presence when you're tired.

But I must keep trying.

Help me.

I love You.

November 11, 1992 — Manchester

My Love,

I'm in the airport lounge waiting for the passport control to Ireland to open. I suppose it will. Otherwise no one will ever get on the plane. You did not intend me to travel, of that I'm sure. At least You didn't give me the physiology of a confirmed gypsy. However, I have not lost my temper once, not even inwardly. Travel is hard work, but it was a lot harder for my grandparents and even harder for the earlier Irish immigrants who were lucky if they lived to get to America.

How cheaply they seemed to have held their lives to run the risk, yet their lives were as dear to them as mine is to me. Perhaps they were only more fatalistic, knowing that they might well die soon either way. Fatalistic but hopeful. Dear God, how much hope must have moved them!

I'm grateful for all the blessings You have given me. Help me to give You something back, You and all those who came before me.

I love You.

November 12, 1992 — Dublin

My Love,

We've had sunshine for two days, for which You are to be most especially thanked, even if You have worked it out through the laws of nature. Two days of sunshine are about all I need to catch up on the jet lag.

While this trip is necessary because of all the sociological consultation which must be done and because of my trip out to the west for my novel, it is still true that Dublin and my friendships here are part of my life and, just as in Arizona, it would be hard for me to give them up. I am grateful to You for giving me the opportunity to return here so often.

I did manage to be patient and pleasant yesterday, even dreamed of it last night, a foolish dream in which I thought I had finally made a change in my life because I had acquired the habit of being aware of Your presence all the time. Well, the dream at any rate shows what I would like to have happen and how I would like to live!

The Northern Ireland negotiations have broken down, which is a bad thing for this country. On the other hand because of the toughness of the Irish negotiator the European trade agreement is back on track. The latter is surely good for the world. But I hope You can finally work out the required graces for peace to come to this island.

There was a story in the paper this morning about a woman beaten to death with baseball bats by a loyalist paramilitary unit because she had violated their ethical standards. That won't make the American papers. Grant rest to her and all others who have suffered in this terrible ongoing conflict.

And help me to continue to do all I can to reflect Your grace and love during this trip.

In particular, if You can arrange it, a third sunny day would be an enormous help.

I love You.

November 13, 1992 — Dublin

My Love,

I read this morning two of Yeats's poems, appropriate for being in Dublin — "Sally Gardens" and "Innisfree." For pure Irish lyricism they are hard to beat. He surely deserved his Nobel prize. But if he had won his love in the Sally Gardens, he would still have been restless and he would not have relaxed at Innisfree either. Such is human nature. I have won my love in a certain sense and Grand Beach is my Innisfree. While both are wonderful, neither is enough to make my heart peaceful and content. Nor are all the achievements and successes of my life enough to satisfy my longings. Here in Ireland, among a certain element of the clergy, I am close to being a folk hero, mostly because I am from "out of town." If I were a native I'd be an outcast just as I am in America. But the admiration is real enough even if it is problematic. It's nice, but it would not content me for long even if I were taken in by it. Life is not about the search for future happiness. It is about the appreciation of present joy. Indeed, and I do appreciate the varied joys of this visit. They all reveal Your presence. But they do not ultimately satisfy, as did not either the Sally Gardens or the Lake Isle. You alone will satisfy me. I know that in my head. Perhaps I am beginning to realize that even in my heart.

I love You. Help me to love You more.

November 14, 1992 — Dublin

My Love,

First rain here, which means it's warming up. I'm grateful for the four days of sun and the quick end of the jet lag.

I read some Irish theology papers yesterday and last night, all good. They emphasized in the words of Vincent MacNamara that Christian ethics must be in line with the Christian story — ethos and mythos consistent with one another. But the Christian story is not one of rules but of forgiving love, as much as Catholic leadership has tried to turn it back to a story of rules. This notion that we are in the grip of Your forgiving love is clear in the preaching of Your Son Jesus and in the parables and in the gospels. How have we made it into a story of negative sexual rules? I think the gap between the theological understanding of what Jesus was about and the posture of the official church is greater than it's ever been, mostly because the official church is more concerned about its own power than it is about Your Son.

Not that my life is any paragon as an example of how one lives when one is taken up by the story of such forgiving love. I have, as You well know, tried to convey this story in my own stories, and occasionally I am angry at those who refuse to see that point even though it is right in front of their eyes. But that's not the issue. The issue is that I have to go a long way to be an adequate disciple of Jesus, and this is not good because I have a pretty clear idea of what that means. I tell the stories but live the stories only in part, for which I am sorry. But Your forgiving love covers even that. Moreover I'm a little better at it than I used to, be for which I am very grateful.

I'm doing okay as the first week of my trip comes to an end, for which I am also very grateful. Help me to hold together for the rest of the adventure.

November 15, 1992 — Dublin

My Love,

I'm off in a couple of hours to Knock and Castlebarr in the County Mayo to visit relatives and sites. I'll be back in Dublin tomorrow afternoon, You and the weather being willing. Take care of me on the trip. Everything is too much rushed, but that's the way of it in my life.

Yeats in the poems I read this morning celebrates his love and mourns her loss and sorrows even that her beauty will pass away. Well does the little book I'm reading call him the "Last Romantic." In fact, such romantic worship of woman or a woman (Maud Gonne in this instance) objectifies the woman and makes her an object for adoring imagination rather than a person to be respected as such and loved as such. Romanticism doesn't permit that, though there are worse kinds of objectification.

I suspect Yeats was happier in the loss of his love than he ever would have been in possession of her, which is also Romantic. I think I would be just the opposite. What fun is it to lose? And if the love turns out to be a limited mortal like yourself, so what? She's probably more loveable in the real world precisely because of her humanity. Goddesses, I suspect, are very hard to live with.

Yet human love, even almost intolerably romantic human love of the Yeats variety, is nothing more than a hunger for You. You are in fact the only appropriate target of romantic love. All the interim romances, as admirable as they may be, are a hint and an anticipation of You. Willie Yeats was hungering for You even though he hardly knew it. And poor Maud was a sacrament of You.

Goddesses are, as I say, hard to live with. But that doesn't apply to You. The difficulty is with me, not with You, though I must confess some of the time You seem a little difficult too! For Your own good reasons, no doubt!

Anyway, we all search for love, we all search to understand love, we all search to be possessed by love. That's a search finally for You, though it does not thereby weaken the importance and the poignancy of human love searches.

Help me to love.

November 17, 1992 — Dublin

My Love,

I had a great time out in Mayo for which many thanks. I reflect on all the suffering and pain, all the tragedy and heartache, all the hunger and death which went before me, from the peaceful Stone-Age farmers living on the north coast of Mayo (where there is nothing between people and the North Pole!) down through the Famine and into even the very near past, and I shudder at so much sorrow. How hard Your love must have to work to dry all the tears and heal all the pain! Good mother that You are, You will, I firmly believe, take care of them all and indeed have taken care of them. But still the tragedy and the pain were all real, the suffering was real, the hardship and the heartache was real. I stand on the shoulders if not of giants at least of many good and faithful people.

The weather continues to comfort, and I continue to enjoy this journey, though I look forward to returning home. This has been a pleasant interlude, not because of any greater maturity on my part but because of good weather, a way around the jet lag, and my own good health — all of which are unmerited blessings.

Yeats this morning has the pensioner spitting on the young people who ignore him because he has his own memories of greatness and love. That's one way to cope with growing old. I prefer the faith I expressed in one of my poems (copies of the book arrived yesterday, as I don't have to tell You!) that we will all be young again and we will laugh again. Youth is a sacrament of the world to come, but so is old age. In Your kingdom, I firmly hope and believe, the vigor and beauty of Youth will be combined with the wisdom of maturity — a combination well worth anticipating!

I'm meeting two real poets this afternoon (separately): Seamus Heaney and Richard Kearney. That should be interesting. Help me to keep my wit and good humor with me till the end of the trip.

I love You.

November 18, 1992 — Dublin

My Love,

The psalmist and Willy Yeats are on the same wave length today. The latter laments for the love who trod on his dreams, and the former says life is short and troubled and we vanish. And so it is. Or so is part of the story anyway. The encounter with both Richard Kearney and Seamus Heaney yesterday opened a flood of images of Ireland and nature and love and You, all of which are whirling around my head in confusion. I should sort this trip out in poems also, but there are already two unfinished ones on disk to which I have paid no attention at all. Nor do I think I will work on them on the way back. Maybe at Thanksgiving time at Grand Beach. Maybe.

Life is troubled and short, but I don't believe we vanish. We know that we are thrust into being by Love. Or at least we suspect that, not being altogether sure. For either there is Love thrusting us and attracting us or it's all blind chance, and even then one must ask the question of how there can be chance.

Or to say the same thing in Jack Shea's words, there is nothing good or loving in the world which is not preserved in Your mind and hence does not die. We survive, though how we do it is something that we are not permitted to know. When I think about that question I find the doubts rise, so I don't think about it too much. The mystery of how we survive is no more answerable than the mystery of how we were launched in the first place. But I do believe.

In any event, this is my last day in Ireland. I leave tomorrow morning for London and Manchester and then home the next day. It will be nice to get home, but this has been a wonderful trip.

Bring me home safely to those I love and who, revealing You, love me. I love You.

November 21, 1992 — Chicago

My Love,

Back home, for which many thanks, and in better shape than I often am when I return from Europe. A mountain of stuff waiting for me. It will take a week to catch up with the pile that was two weeks building. I will put off my work on the reader till the first week in Advent. I also must lose lots of weight, which will be difficult, I ate too much while I was away.

It's good to be home, so good, even though the trip went well.

Nice quote from Harper today: "It is not true there is a God but he doesn't care about us. What is true is that if God does not care about us than it's not God!"

I like that and I believe that and I love You.

November 22, 1992 — Chicago

My Love,

It is a month and three days before the Feast of the Birth of Your Son. Already the lights are aglow on the Magnificent Mile just below me. This afternoon after the Bears lose another I will put up my Christmas tree. I'm already playing Christmas music on the stereo. You know how much I appreciate this season and also how the Christmas ethos gets lost for me in the compounding of my ordinary work demands and the meals and parties I must attend. I hope this year to concentrate a little more on the meaning of the festival — the light winning out over the darkness, which could not put it out.

Against the low gray clouds that hang over the city this morning the lights in my apartment stand out brilliantly. So do the trees below on Michigan Avenue. So does the hope You offer in a grim and suffering world.

Grant that in this season of hope and joy I may remember that I am one of those invited by You to be the light of the world and to shed my light on all who come near me.

November 23, 1992 — Chicago

My Love,

I have begun to *reread* for my Christmastime reading Jack Shea's book *Starlight*, a wonderful book. Christmas is a festival which defies the weather, at least in the Northern Hemisphere. Shakespeare has some lovely lines about the bird of dawning that sings all night at the time of Our Lord's birth. Night, Jack says, is the context for "starlight." You only appreciate the light *because* there is darkness. Night is good too in itself, especially the night this time of the year when it is permeated by a certain kind of light, a soft, private, reassuring light. Night is filled with wonder and surprise. No telling who we will meet. Sometimes there is terror, but sometimes there is also love waiting for us.

Chicago was incredibly gray yesterday, the trees stripped of their leaves, Buckingham Fountain dry, the Bears empty, fog obscuring the skyline, clouds seeming to hang just above the trees. Dark, dank, empty, but also somehow sacramental, perhaps because of the hint that this barrenness is not final, that fallow does not mean dead, that stark does not mean lifeless. Or perhaps because one knows that the process of life and light goes on even in the darkness and thus transforms the darkness itself even when as yesterday there was so little light.

We do make a lot of the precession of the earth on its wobbly axis, don't we? A small bump in the way a tiny planet rotates and we turn it into symbols of life and death, good and evil, hope and despair.

But if You are the one You claim to be, no planet is unimportant and no sign is without meaning. So in seeing the seasons as sacraments we're doing what You want us to do. In the paradox of light and darkness (and there can be too much light too) we see hints of what life means and therefore rejoice with tree and candles and fruits and music and the scent of evergreen.

November 24, 1992 — Chicago

My Love,

At the dinner party last night for Jack Shea and Jack Egan, the former said, with the usual calm and quiet confidence that marks his insights, "God doesn't punish." There were some challenges to it and I was caught up in another conversation and didn't hear all the details. But of course he was right. You don't punish. You pursue each of us with forgiving love, recklessly, relentlessly, with cunning and determination, with passion and skill, with implacable energy and tender delicacy, with grim insistence and infinite patience.

Patently.

Yet not so patently that, even two thousand years after the coming of Your Son, those who claim to be his followers have really caught on. So much of our concern focuses on forcing others to do what we want them to do in the name, of course, of what we claim You want them to do and then punishing them when they don't act right. For how many priests has this been the purpose of their lives. And for how long a time it took me to realize that the game isn't played that way.

And I have yet to learn that I should not want to punish those who have done harm to me. I don't punish them of course, but the impulse is there and allowed to persist and fester all too often.

As I give thanks this weekend help me to understand that the most important gift for which to be thankful is Your forgiving love.

And to love You in return.

November 25, 1992 — Grand Beach

My Love,

I've come up here for the Thanksgiving celebration. There have been twenty-three sunless days this month and apparently this will continue through the weekend. The weather was better in Dublin.

I want to reflect today on an incident on Saturday night when I was driving home. Despite the drizzle and the fog, construction was taking place on the Kennedy, with lanes confused by barriers. At Division Street a driver, confused and impatient — and possibly drunk — lurched from the ramp broadside in front of me. Despite the slippery pavement, my brakes worked and, thank You very much, there was no car behind me. Hence there was no pile-up. Then the driver in front of me turned off a half minute latter at Ogden. He put his life at risk and mine and others who might have been behind me for a half mile ride!

As I say he was either a fool or drunk or, if the latter, both.

But it reminds me or the fragility of life, of my life. Death can be so causal, so accidental, so much the result of chance and stupidity. My life hangs by a thread. I know that of course. I read the papers. I know what happens to others can happen to me. How many other brushes with death do I survive without even noticing them. The odds are against it at any given time, but death can always await me — random, needless, capricious, senseless (as the papers say) death.

I can't say my life passed before my eyes on Saturday night; there was no time for that. All I thought was of the possibility of a car behind me as I put on the brakes. There was a moment of fear and then it was over and nothing happened — the initial state I suppose of an accident with the rest of the process, for which thank You, cut off.

Transient, fragile, problematic, that's the nature of my life. I am grateful for that life and for all the excitement and adventure it has involved. I am grateful for Your protection from disaster (even if I don't and never will understand the mystery of Your providence) and I accept whatever death might occur to me (however fearfully) because I know that even death will not separate me from Your love.

November 26, 1992, Thanksgiving Day — Grand Beach

My Love,

I talked to Jack yesterday and got some more insights on You not punishing. I must say it was an interesting counterpoint to the book I was reading on canon law and sex by Brundage. How did we ever get so confused, so completely off the track?

But, it being Thanksgiving, I wish to give thanks for all the good things with which You've blessed me, none of which I have merited or deserved:

My life, my health, my priesthood, my family and friends, those who love me and whom I love, the imperfect church though the best there is, the glorious Catholic tradition, the freedom and prosperity of my country, my abilities, the excitement of my life, my recent renewals with the cardinal and the university, the challenges and opportunities which continue to come my way. Grand Beach, Tucson, my trip to Ireland, and all the other good things which You have given me.

A short list, but even as short it's incredible. Pondering as I have in my poetry the last several days the Céide fields people, my cousins and ancestors, I realize how much I owe them and how much more I have than they did. I don't deserve it and I don't understand it, but I am still grateful for all You have given me, but most of all for Your love, in which I want to place my total confidence and trust.

November 27, 1992 — Grand Beach

My Love,

The key to the story of the woman taken in adultery is that Jesus wrote on the ground with his finger twice, just as You are described as writing the law on the stone tablets with Your finger twice and the second time promising Moses forgiveness and love for ten thousand generations (250,000 years if it is to be taken literally which of course it isn't). In the story Your forgiveness and love are specified as applying not only to a people in general but to people in particular. That's the way God is, the artfully crafted story tells us.

Mercy and forgiveness for ten thousand generations!

How badly the church has understood that You don't punish, and neither should it punish! How long will it take us to understand that truth? Dear God, how horrible is the lust for power in the church and how badly it has disfigured Your love for all of us.

Somehow I must make that theme in the writing which is ahead of me. I already push forgiveness, as is obvious in *Fall from Grace,* but the punitiveness of the church, that needs more emphasis. Yet there must be mercy and forgiveness even for the church leaders who have obscured and disfigured Your love.

The truth in the story should never be forgotten: God does not punish!

And God is also insidiously clever in persuading humans to return love. How hard sometimes You have to work at it.

November 28, 1992 — Chicago

My Love,

Back in Chicago for the beginning of Advent tomorrow. In *Starlight* I read about how important all the things around Christmas are for reminding us that it is indeed Christmas, an opportunity not to be missed. As I do my shopping and attend all the parties, I must remember what is happening. I also must fast, which means moderate eating and no drinking and no desserts unless there are hostess problems. And I also must do some special Christmas prayers, perhaps at the beginning and end of each day when I bounce in and out of bed. It would be a good habit and it would remind me that Jesus, Your Son, has come into the world to bring hope and light and peace.

Jack describes exactly how I feel at Christmas. I believe in the festival and in all the festivities but I grow weary and forget about it as I am dragged around — and this despite all the Christmas paraphernalia with which I surround myself. Help me to do a little better this year.

Thank You for the weekend in Grand Beach. I love You very much.

November 29, 1992 — Chicago

My Love,

Jack writes about gifts in the passage I've just read. What is the most memorable kind of Christmas gift? One that represents the honest and intense love of another. No doubt about that. I spend a lot of money on gifts and sometimes buy them in mass-production form. But the gifts I'm giving are nice and they come from affection. And as long as I have the money to spend there is no reason not to be generous. But I must not let the giving become routine. I must treasure each gift and the giving and the one to whom I give it.

Help me to keep that in mind during the next couple of joyous weeks.

I love You, the greatest giver of all.

November 30, 1992 — Chicago

My Love,

I note that the "Reverend Grinches" are trying to steal Christmas. A group of clerics, including alas some of our own, are decrying the "commercialism" of Christmas. It's hard to know what they mean by that phrase — advertising and merchandising I guess — but they are against it. They want Christmas to be "austere." How's that for missing the point completely? Christmas isn't supposed to be austere; it's supposed to be an exuberant explosion of love and joy over the return of light and the coming of the Light of the World. Austerity is not an appropriate response.

Doubtless some people miss the point. Doubtless a lot of us get worn out and battered. Doubtless some merchants are interested only in making money — though it does not follow that the gifts we buy from them are thereby tainted. Doubtless some gifts are less than sincere. But that does not mean that gifts are not an important part of Christmas, a powerful reminder, if we permit them to be, of what Christmas is. Moreover if people don't buy Christmas gifts the economy will plunge into a deeper abyss and lots of people, especially poor people, will lose their jobs.

They use the ultimate weapon of the grinches these days. They warn us about pollution. We are destroying the planet by giving Christmas gifts. Come on, guys! Christmas gift-wrapping is surely biodegradable and it can be recycled anyway.

Spoilsports!

There is finally no necessary relationship between giving gifts and savoring what Christmas is about. The relationship can go either way, depending on what we do with the exchange of gifts. Austerity does not necessarily welcome the Jesus baby. One thing it does do, however, is generate a feeling of moral superiority in those who practice it which is totally against the spirit of Christmas.

Well! I've delivered myself of that harangue. It now behooves me with Your help to show that exuberance is appropriate for Christmas. I must not let myself get tired.

Help me this Christmas.

On this feast of my patron, I want to say that I love You especially much — You should excuse my exuberant English!

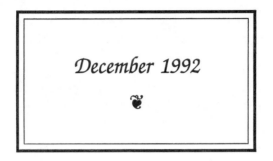

December 1992

December 1, 1992 — Chicago

My Love,

Today begins the last month of the year. It's two months since I returned from Grand Beach. I have squeezed a frantic amount of activity into the two months. I've survived pretty well and have not been bone-tired like I usually am this time of the year. But now it all seems to be catching up with me. Or maybe it's the endlessly gray skies or the clogged sinuses every morning. Anyway I don't want to be a basket case all December long. I'm not sure how to respond. Maybe I should suspend all work at some point and just loaf. I've earned that, I suppose. As my niece Liz pointed out over the Thanksgiving weekend there is no break between work and rest in my life, none at all. Maybe I should say that a vacation starts the week before Christmas. That might just make a lot of sense.

In Jack's book these days he writes about reflection on experience. In my own models of reflection I have seen it as a critique, a move by individual or institution from the first to the second naiveté. That must be done, of course, and is not unimportant. But Jack points at another and more important function of reflection: It opens up the consciousness to further possibilities based on the insights of the original experience. Reflection opens the self to new possibilities of seeing and living. It integrates the preexperience personality with the experience and reorders the configuration with which the person faces the world. Reflection makes the experience a permanent part of the personality.

That's neat and certainly true in my own life. Thus my poem on the autumn moon becomes a permanent part of my attitude about the moon and shapes my new perceptions of that heavenly body, making it more graceful to me than it was before the experience and before I recorded the experience in verse.

Thank You for the wonderful complexity of the human personality. I love You.

December 2, 1992 — Chicago

My Love,

Someone spoke to me last night at her horror at seeing a homeless woman who seemed to be living in the women's room at a shopping mall. That person was once a baby beloved by her mother, once a girl with bright dreams, once a young woman with eager hopes for her life. Now she has no one and no place. It doesn't seem fair.

I tried to persuade my friend that she was not responsible for this woman's plight, that her good Christmas did not cause the other woman a bad Christmas, that voting for a Democratic president was a good step towards dealing with the homeless problem, the scope of which is exaggerated anyway.

All these things are true. Yet there ought not to be a single homeless person in our society. They move us deeply even if there is little directly we can do for them. Moreover, the question always arises, as it did for my friend last night, as to why You permit such tragedy. There is no answer, no answer to all the death one sees in this morning's paper. We must believe that You love that poor woman as much as You love any of Your children. We must believe that eventually You will take care of her and wipe away all her tears.

Yet somehow, while that's all we can say, it seems too little, particularly at this time of the year. I want to eliminate all the suffering in the world. So, I must believe, do You. But it must not be easy or You would have done it long ago.

I'm baffled. I must do something more this Christmas. I have been generous. I must find a way to be more generous. Help me to see where I can make a contribution.

December 3, 1992 — Chicago

My Love,

In my reading from *Starlight* this morning I see that one must put oneself in the way of everyday sacraments to be absorbed by the spirit of Christmas. One must listen to the music, smell the scent, revel in the lights, enjoy the gift-giving. One must be into Christmas "in a big way." That's difficult for me because I am juggling so many different projects and responsibilities. I am indeed surrounded by the paraphernalia of Christmas, but I have a lunch at the Lyric and a symphony tonight and my collection of readings to finish and the phone to answer and the Christmas stuff is at most background music and of course I'll have to go to the dentist next week.

I must have time to contemplate to "get in the way" of Christmas — or any other sacrament. Left to myself, every day will be the same, a grind of work, responsibilities, and phone calls. I do plan to stop working a week before Christmas but I wonder if I can really pull that off. I think I've done it before, and the project fizzled. I'll need Your help to do it.

For so much of my life I've worked and missed the point of life. No, that's not true or fair. I have taken time off. I do understand the point of life, but I still tend to get caught up in the daily grind, from the moment I get out of bed in the morning until I collapse at the end of the day — especially when the phone starts to ring.

If it makes trouble today I will definitely use call forward.

Weird, isn't it, my love, to scapegoat an electronic device? The heart of the matter is the people who use it, and they are *You* coming to me through the voices of troubled brothers and sisters. So I must listen to them too — but not necessarily every moment of the day. Help me through this maze. I love You.

December 4, 1992 — Chicago

My Love,

The trick of understanding Christmas, Jack says in the passage I read this morning, is to see reality with a "third eye." Well, to be fair, he doesn't advance this as his opinion but rather as the opinion of spiritual teachers.

It is certainly true that we must penetrate beyond appearances to reality, though I am always skeptical of those who claim that they know what the reality is because there is moral righteousness in that position that needs the hermeneutic of suspicion.

However, the trick is to try to see the reality for yourself and not try to impose it on others. Or to put it another way, the secret is to appreciate the surface and understand the depth. It ain't easy, to put it mildly. We live on the surface, we are bugged by the surface, we are distracted by the surface, our friends and lovers encounter us on the surface. It takes time, which we often don't have, to break away from the surface.

Last night I heard music about the resurrection at Orchestra Hall, good Christmas music too. No strings, just winds and horns and percussion. Triumphant music. It made me sense momentarily what the world is like beneath the surface. Yet no time to think or reflect or — what I think is necessary for the third eye faculty to work — to sink oneself into the sacramentality of the music — something I do only when I write poems.

All the more reason to declare a moratorium on work starting on Monday, December 14. Then I will turn loose the third eye. If I can. I know from other such attempts that it doesn't work very well. But I can try.

And maybe a little bit before then.

I love You. Help me to see!

December 5, 1992 — Chicago

My Love,

You don't have to go to Bethlehem to see where Jesus was born. For the Christmas event happens inside us. So Jack says in this morning's reading. And of course he is correct. Jesus comes at Christmas in the personality of each one of us. We are shocked out of our ordinary life by strange stories — wise men, virgin births, God become human, a king in the tomb — and forced to reconsider what life means and what we are doing with our life.

They are wonder stories and they are designed to open our minds and hearts once more to wonder — the wonder of birth, the wonder of love, the wonder of light in the darkness. Perhaps the worst thing which can happen to us humans is to lose our wonder. That is a sign of old age (and it can happen at twenty-five), of deterioration, of collapse of that which is most authentically human in us.

The sun shines this morning, though I guess it is cold outside. But the city and the lake and the neighborhoods glow in the early morning light. Wonderful! Full of wonder. And if You are the Wonder of them all, then the city glows with You.

Thank You for the wonder! Help my sense of it to grow and flourish this Christmas time.

I love You.

December 6, 1992 — Chicago

My Love,

A low, grim sky stretches out to the west over the city. Snow in the forecast. The other day when snowflakes were falling at the university, Dave Tracy said, "How beautiful." And I said, "Not if you have to drive in it." Both of us were right. The big, lazy flakes were beautiful, but I dread Christmas driving in the snow, particularly with all the drunks who are on the road.

I remember — how can I ever forget — the car which turned over just as I passed it in a blizzard on the Kennedy. I couldn't even stop in the rush of traffic. I pray for the people in the car, living or dead. But I still shiver every time I see that image. Death in the snow at Christmas! Especially if it is the result of someone else's drunkenness! Ugh!

I'll be out much of the day. Mass, visits, parties. I'd rather not rush around just yet, not until I clean up my pre-Christmas work. But I must not be a party pooper. I should try to radiate the wonder of the season and be a wonder-full person. Not easy, but maybe it should be easy. If it's not easy, it's not wonder.

Stay with me, please, and take care of me through this season.

I love You.

December 7, 1992 — Chicago

My Love,

Christmas is above all a festival of life that we celebrate this time of the year, superabundant life, overflowing life, more life than we can possibly use or comprehend. I must convey this to people through my own vitality through the stories I tell at Mass about life.

This morning I don't feel very lively — gloomy Monday, clogged sinuses. And too much food. Yet, as I found in the liturgy yesterday, one can come alive regardless of how one feels.

When I was through working last night about 9:30, I turned on TV to see if anything was happening. No surprises. But I did encounter two clergymen, one of ours and one of theirs. Both were warning of hellfire and evil. They were so far from where I am religiously that it seemed we were hardly in the same tradition. Not much trace of life or of love in either of them. To them You are a God of wrath and punishment, almost reluctant to spoil humans with too much love. I don't know how we got into this approach, but it is certainly widespread and it has little to do with Jesus and the gospels and the Christmas message. The Protestant clergyman was an old-fashioned hell-fire type, rigid, punitive. The Catholic was a Polish priest, warm and fatherly in manner — dressed in a cassock with a cross in the sash — but just as punitive in the religion he preached. It doesn't seem unfair to say that they and their ilk still dominate the public image of Christianity. It's no surprise that people like my novels with their different emphasis.

I don't know what the conclusion of this is. Just that I must preach Your love all the more vigorously whenever I get a chance.

Help me to do so. I love You.

December 8, 1992 — Chicago

My Love,

So much death yesterday. Bosnian women raped and then murdered by Serbs. Forty killed in Somalia. Hundreds killed in Muslim-Hindu riots in India. Israeli soldiers killed by Arabs.

On and on and on. Just another day on planet earth. Each death an individual human tragedy. Each one a terrible act of dehumanization by the killers.

How frail and vulnerable are the lives of Your children!

Such terrible suffering for Your children! Such suffering for You if indeed You suffer with us as You say You do. When will it ever end? I guess the answer is that it never will, not until Your kingdom finally comes and just now it seems a long way off.

I pray for them all, each of them, that You wipe away their tears and bring them peace and happiness.

Every time I think of these things I feel helpless, wanting to do something and unable to stop any of it. I understand the reaction of the relief workers in Somalia who want the United States to come and make everything right, almost as though the U.S. is You with infinite powers to do everything. Obviously we can't, and just as obviously we're trying to play that role again. Well, maybe this time we'll get away with it, but it looks more like hubris than charity.

A gray grim day and gray grim thoughts. Snow in the air. I'm to read poems tonight at Waterstone's book store and I'm wary of it. I should never have agreed to do it in the first place. Well, too late to be prudent now.

Anyway I love You. Help me to love You more. Help me to be cheerful with the joy of Christmas, even at the dentist's this morning.

December 9, 1992 — Chicago

My Love,

In the chapter I read this morning in Jack's book he tells the story of Adam and Eve and the manger and then explains it. I like the story better than any explanation, but that's the way it is with stories.

The point of the story, as I see it, is that Adam and Eve are resisting the burdens and constraints of being human and learn from Jesus the sanctity and the goodness of being human.

I guess I need to learn that myself. My sinuses are blocked, my stomach is upset, my teeth are not right, I am tired, and the gray sky depresses me.

That's being human with a vengeance, isn't it?

Not as bad as a lot of people, for sure; all minor ailments, but enough to tie me down, burden me, constrain and impede my enthusiasm and joy.

The poetry reading went well last night, but I was tense and depressed afterwards and the slow meal service made me even more tense. The dinner should have been fun, I thought it would be fun, but it wasn't — not for me.

I'm not sure about the others because I may have been reading my tension into them. Bad scene and in substantial part my own fault.

I feel that I need one good night's sleep, but I have been sleeping well.

I don't know.

Anyway I make my point: I am constrained by my body, just like Adam and Eve in the story. And I should rejoice in that body? If Jesus shared the human body and its constraints and limitations than the body is good and I should rejoice — despite my sinuses and the burdens of Christmas eating.

Did Jesus have a sinus problem?

How terrible to get hung up on something so minor.

I'll be better soon. The soporific effect of the sinus pill will wear off.

What I'm trying to get at is that You love me anyway, and that is all that matters just now. If You are patient with me, then I must be patient with myself.

I love You.

December 31, 1992 — Chicago

My Love,

You and I both know that it's not the end of 1992 today at all but June 18, 1993. However, Your good servant Mike Leach who edits these books (and does a wonderfully skilled job) asked me to send him the rest of December. I was forced to tell him that the computer ate those reflections (perhaps just as well, perhaps it knew what it was doing) and that, while You probably remembered them (since You remember everything), I didn't. So he asked me to try to put together a last-day-of-the-year reflection after I had gone through his editing to make sure that he had cut everything that ought to be cut (materials which might injure others and repetitions).

As You know, I find it painful to read these reflections. I gave up on trying to read them a day at a time last year. I don't understand why anyone else would want to read them, but people do and if it helps their prayer to You I am willing to share my reflections with anyone who is interested.

Of the second volume, some friends observed that I had been very tired, and it had been a hard year. In this third volume, I think as I flip the pages, I am still tired but it was a much more interesting and blessed year. For that I'm very grateful. I am also grateful for my reconciliation with both the university and the cardinal, which happened last year but which have grown and flourished this year. I am very grateful indeed for the favorable reactions of the students to my course in the student book I just received.

You take good care of me despite me. You really must love me. You take care of all of us, each in our own way, each as an individual which, I take it, is the story the angels tell.

As I have said to You before, I do not find the man in these pages all that attractive. The reviewers of the first two volumes apparently did, as apparently did the readers, though the books have yet to fall into the hands of those who really hate me. I shudder at the thought of what the *Commonweal* types will do when and if they finally notice these books.

In any case the reflections are written for You. I think I have been able to keep possible publication out of my head as I write them and that they are authentic prayers. Well, mostly authentic, since nothing human is ever completely authentic. And You like me whatever might be my faults. Indeed, You love me. That is the only consideration I should have in these reflections and it is, I think, the dominant reflection.

So as I try to put myself back in the post-Christmas mood last December, I am sorry for all my faults and mistakes, grateful to You for all the gifts with which You have blessed me in superabundance during the last years, and especially thankful for all the signs of love which have overwhelmed me through my life.

One of my agnostic friends wondered why I had to tell You that I loved You everyday. That's what lovers do, don't they?

I love You.